SQL Practice Problems

57 beginning, intermediate, and advanced challenges for you to solve using a "learn-by-doing" approach

Sylvia Moestl Vasilik

Table of Contents

How to use this book

This book assumes that you have some basic background knowledge about relational databases. However, I've added some beginner level questions to gradually introduce the various parts of the SQL Select statement for those with less experience in SQL.

A note on the database used: it is *not* the standard Northwind database that was the sample included with several Microsoft database products. There have been many changes made to it, including additional tables, and modified data, to support the problems in this book. Do not try to use the standard Northwind sample database, many of the problems will not work.

Do you need to finish *all* the problems?

Absolutely not. The introductory problems are fairly simple, so you may want to skip directly to the Intermediate Problems section. If you're not a beginner, but not sure where you should start, look at the problems and expected results in the Introductory Problems section, and make sure you completely understand the concepts and answers. Then try skipping to the Intermediate problems.

If you're uncertain about how to start on a problem, the hints are designed to gradually walk you through how to approach the problem. Try hard to solve the problems first without the hints! But if you're stuck, the hints will get you started.

Should you look at the answers in the back of the book?

Not unless absolutely necessary. If possible, avoid looking at the answers and discussion section until you've solved the problem to the best of your ability. You will learn and remember much more. And if possible, try not even looking at the hints unless you're stuck.

But searching online for code syntax and examples is a good idea, and often necessary. I expect you to research online as you work through the problems. I do not include all the syntax in this book. In my day-to-day work as a data engineer, I would be lost without being able to do online research. Sometimes I search online for a reminder of a certain syntax, sometimes for examples of a particular type of code, and sometimes for approaches to specific problems. Learning to find answers online effectively can cut your problem-solving time dramatically.

Once you finish all the questions, you'll have some extremely useful skills in data analysis and data mining. The ability to use SQL is the foundation of data engineering, and (thankfully) does not change very frequently at all. This is useful because the SQL that you learned 10 years ago will probably be just as useful 10 years in the future! And it's a relatively rare skill. I've interviewed many people who rated themselves a "9 or 10" on a 1-10 scale of SQL knowledge, who could not even do a simple Group by in a SQL statement.

Select statements aren't all there is to SQL, of course. There's also the syntax that lets you modify data (update, insert, delete), and create and modify database objects), as well as programming concepts such as stored procedures, and of course many other topics.

In this book, I'm only presenting problems involving retrieving data with Select statements, because that's by far the most common need. And it's also an area where it's very difficult for people to get solid practice with real-life data problems, unless they're already working as a data engineer or programmer. Plus, it's a critical first step for almost any other database topics.

Thank you for purchasing this book! Any feedback would be greatly appreciated. For any questions or issues, please send email to feedback@SQLPracticeProblems.com and I will be happy to respond.

Setup

This section will help you install Microsoft SQL Server 2017 Express Edition and SQL Server Management Studio (SSMS). It will also walk you through setting up the practice database.

The setup of Microsoft SQL Server 2017 and SSMS will take about 30 minutes, mostly hands-off. It may require one or two reboots of your system, depending on which version of certain support files you have (such as the .NET framework). SQL Server 2017 will run with more recent versions of Windows, including Windows 8 and Windows 10.

Microsoft SQL Server 2019 became available in late 2019. All the practice problems have been thoroughly tested in SQL Server 2019, so if you choose to install that version, feel free to do so. But it's not required. Most companies and organizations lag behind many years when upgrading their database systems, so Microsoft SQL Server 2017 and earlier versions will be used for a very long time.   .

Setup Steps

1. Install Microsoft SQL Server Express Edition

Download and install MS SQL Server Express Edition 2017 (https://www.microsoft.com/en-cy/sql-server/sql-server-editions-express). It's a free download, and the Express Edition, (unlike the Developer Edition, also free), doesn't require you to sign up for any email lists or subscriptions. Feel free to do the Basic install unless you have special requirements.

Note: if you already have SQL Server 2012 or later installed, and don't want to install SQL Server 2017, you don't need to. All of the SQL functionality used in this book is included in SQL Server 2012.

2. Install SQL Server Management Studio

Download and install SQL Server Management Studio (SSMS) (https://docs.microsoft.com/en-us/sql/ssms/sql-server-management-studio-ssms?view=sql-server-2017).

This is the tool that allows you to interact with SQL Server, to write SQL and browse the objects.

You can either do this as a part of the MS SQL Server Express Edition 2017 install (there's a link at the bottom), or download it directly, after you finish the MS SQL Server Express Edition install.

3. Set up the practice database

You'll be using a SQL script file to set up the practice database. To download the SQL script file, go to https://sqlpracticeproblems.com/Resources. Click on the link and download the zip file.

When you expand the zip file, you'll find the SQL script file called SQLPracticeProblems_SQLServer_PracticeDBSetup.sql. It will create the tables and data needed to solve the practice problems.

This walk-through video shows you the exact steps needed to run the script file:

https://youtu.be/u62uD1RHRv4

Questions or problems with the setup?
Please email me at feedback@SQLPracticeProblems.com

Database diagram for practice database

A database diagram is a visualization of all the tables, fields, and relationships in a database. It can help you understand how the tables are related to each other.

This is the database diagram for the Northwind_SPP practice database we will be using.

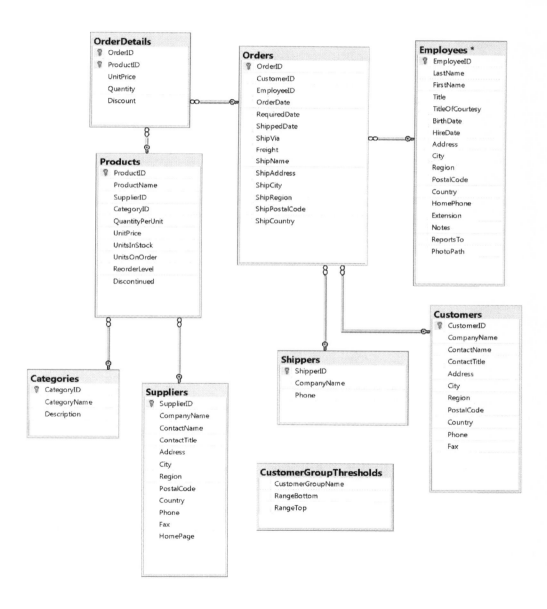

Introductory Problems

1. Which shippers do we have?

We have a table called Shippers. Return all the fields from all the shippers

Expected Results

ShipperID	CompanyName	Phone
1	Speedy Express	(503) 555-9831
2	United Package	(503) 555-3199
3	Federal Shipping	(503) 555-9931

Hint

The standard format for a select statement that returns all columns and all rows is "Select * from TableName".

2. Certain fields from Categories

In the Categories table, selecting all the fields using this SQL:

```
Select * from Categories
```

...will return 4 columns. We only want to see two columns, CategoryName and Description.

Expected Results

CategoryName	Description
Beverages	Soft drinks, coffees, teas, beers, and ales
Condiments	Sweet and savory sauces, relishes, spreads, and seasonings
Confections	Desserts, candies, and sweet breads
Dairy Products	Cheeses
Grains/Cereals	Breads, crackers, pasta, and cereal
Meat/Poultry	Prepared meats

Produce	Dried fruit and bean curd
Seafood	Seaweed and fish

Hint

Instead of * in the Select statement, specify the column names with a comma between them.

3.   Sales Representatives

We'd like to see just the FirstName, LastName, and HireDate of all the employees with the title of Sales Representative. Write a SQL statement that returns only those employees.

Expected Results

FirstName	LastName	HireDate
Nancy	Davolio	2010-05-01 00:00:00.000
Janet	Leverling	2010-04-01 00:00:00.000
Margaret	Peacock	2011-05-03 00:00:00.000
Michael	Suyama	2011-10-17 00:00:00.000
Robert	King	2012-01-02 00:00:00.000
Anne	Dodsworth	2012-11-15 00:00:00.000

Hint

To filter out only certain rows from a table, use a Where clause. The format for a where clause with a string filter is:

```
Where
    FieldName = 'Filter Text'
```

4.   Sales Representatives in the United States

Now we'd like to see the same columns as above, but only for those employees that both have the title of Sales Representative, and also are in the United States.

Expected Results

FirstName	LastName	HireDate
Nancy	Davolio	2010-05-01 00:00:00.000
Janet	Leverling	2010-04-01 00:00:00.000
Margaret	Peacock	2011-05-03 00:00:00.000

Hint

To apply multiple filters in a where clause, use "and" to separate the filters.

5.   Orders placed by specific EmployeeID

Show all the orders placed by a specific employee. The EmployeeID for this Employee (Steven Buchanan) is 5.

Expected Results

OrderID	OrderDate
10248	2014-07-04 08:00:00.000
10254	2014-07-11 02:00:00.000
10269	2014-07-31 00:00:00.000
10297	2014-09-04 21:00:00.000
10320	2014-10-03 12:00:00.000
10333	2014-10-18 18:00:00.000
10358	2014-11-20 05:00:00.000
10359	2014-11-21 14:00:00.000
10372	2014-12-04 10:00:00.000
10378	2014-12-10 00:00:00.000
10397	2014-12-27 17:00:00.000
10463	2015-03-04 13:00:00.000
10474	2015-03-13 16:00:00.000
10477	2015-03-17 02:00:00.000

10529	2015-05-07 01:00:00.000
10549	2015-05-27 03:00:00.000
10569	2015-06-16 15:00:00.000
10575	2015-06-20 22:00:00.000
10607	2015-07-22 09:00:00.000

(some result rows were not included; the total should be 42)

Hint

The EmployeeID is an integer field, and not a string field. So, the value "5" does not need to be surrounded by single quotes in the where clause.

6.   Suppliers and ContactTitles

In the Suppliers table, show the SupplierID, ContactName, and ContactTitle for those Suppliers whose ContactTitle is *not* Marketing Manager.

Expected Results

SupplierID	ContactName	ContactTitle
1	Charlotte Cooper	Purchasing Manager
2	Shelley Burke	Order Administrator
3	Regina Murphy	Sales Representative
5	Antonio del Valle Saavedra	Export Administrator
6	Mayumi Ohno	Marketing Representative
8	Peter Wilson	Sales Representative
9	Lars Peterson	Sales Agent
11	Petra Winkler	Sales Manager
12	Martin Bein	International Marketing Mgr.
13	Sven Petersen	Coordinator Foreign Markets
14	Elio Rossi	Sales Representative
16	Cheryl Saylor	Regional Account Rep.
17	Michael Björn	Sales Representative
18	Guylène Nodier	Sales Manager
19	Robb Merchant	Wholesale Account Agent
20	Chandra Leka	Owner
21	Niels Petersen	Sales Manager
22	Dirk Luchte	Accounting Manager

23	Anne Heikkonen	Product Manager
24	Wendy Mackenzie	Sales Representative
26	Giovanni Giudici	Order Administrator
27	Marie Delamare	Sales Manager
28	Eliane Noz	Sales Representative
29	Chantal Goulet	Accounting Manager

Hint

To learn how to do the "not", you can search online for SQL comparison operators.

7. Products with "queso" in ProductName

In the products table, we'd like to see the ProductID and ProductName for those products where the ProductName includes the string "queso".

Expected Results

ProductID	ProductName
11	Queso Cabrales
12	Queso Manchego La Pastora

Hint

In an earlier problem, we were looking for exact matches—where our filter matched the value in the field exactly. Here, we're looking for rows where the ProductName field has the value "queso" somewhere in it.

Use the "like" operator, with wildcards, in the answer. Feel free to do some research online to find examples.

8. Orders shipping to France or Belgium

Looking at the Orders table, there's a field called ShipCountry. Write a query that shows the OrderID, CustomerID, and ShipCountry for the orders where the ShipCountry is either France or Belgium.

Expected Results

OrderID	CustomerID	ShipCountry
10248	VINET	France
10251	VICTE	France
10252	SUPRD	Belgium
10265	BLONP	France
10274	VINET	France
10295	VINET	France
10297	BLONP	France
10302	SUPRD	Belgium
10311	DUMON	France
10331	BONAP	France
10334	VICTE	France
10340	BONAP	France
10350	LAMAI	France
10358	LAMAI	France
10360	BLONP	France
10362	BONAP	France
10371	LAMAI	France

(Some rows were not included; the total should be 96)

Hint

In the where clause, instead of combining the filters with "and", use "or".

9.   Orders shipping to any country in Latin America

Now, instead of just wanting to return all the orders from France or Belgium, we want to show all the orders from any Latin American country. But we don't have a list of Latin American countries in a table in the Northwind database. So, we're going to just use this list of Latin American countries that happen to be in the Orders table:

Brazil
Mexico
Argentina
Venezuela

It doesn't make sense to use multiple Or statements anymore. Use the In statement.

OrderID	CustomerID	ShipCountry
10250	HANAR	Brazil
10253	HANAR	Brazil
10256	WELLI	Brazil
10257	HILAA	Venezuela
10259	CENTC	Mexico
10261	QUEDE	Brazil
10268	GROSR	Venezuela
10276	TORTU	Mexico
10283	LILAS	Venezuela
10287	RICAR	Brazil
10290	COMMI	Brazil
10291	QUEDE	Brazil
10292	TRADH	Brazil
10293	TORTU	Mexico
10296	LILAS	Venezuela
10299	RICAR	Brazil
10304	TORTU	Mexico
10308	ANATR	Mexico
10319	TORTU	Mexico
10322	PERIC	Mexico
10330	LILAS	Venezuela
10347	FAMIA	Brazil
10354	PERIC	Mexico
10357	LILAS	Venezuela

(Some rows were not included, the total should be 173)

Here's an example of the previous questions, about orders shipping to France or Belgium, done as an In statement instead of using multiple Where clauses.

```
Select
    OrderID
    ,CustomerID
    ,OrderDate
```

```
    ,ShipCountry
From Orders
where
    ShipCountry in ('France','Belgium')
```

10. Employees, in order of age

For all the employees in the Employees table, show the FirstName, LastName, Title, and BirthDate. Order the results by BirthDate, so we have the oldest employees first.

Expected Results

FirstName	LastName	Title	BirthDate
Margaret	Peacock	Sales Representative	1955-09-19 00:00:00.000
Nancy	Davolio	Sales Representative	1966-12-08 00:00:00.000
Andrew	Fuller	Vice President, Sales	1970-02-19 00:00:00.000
Steven	Buchanan	Sales Manager	1973-03-04 00:00:00.000
Laura	Callahan	Inside Sales Coordinator	1976-01-09 00:00:00.000
Robert	King	Sales Representative	1978-05-29 00:00:00.000
Michael	Suyama	Sales Representative	1981-07-02 00:00:00.000
Janet	Leverling	Sales Representative	1981-08-30 00:00:00.000
Anne	Dodsworth	Sales Representative	1984-01-27 00:00:00.000

Hint

You'll need to use the Order by clause here for sorting the results. Look online for examples.

11. Showing only the Date with a DateTime field

In the output of the query above, showing the Employees in order of BirthDate, we see the time of the BirthDate field, which we don't want. Show only the date portion of the BirthDate field.

Expected Results

FirstName	LastName	Title	DateOnlyBirthDate
Margaret	Peacock	Sales Representative	1955-09-19
Nancy	Davolio	Sales Representative	1966-12-08
Andrew	Fuller	Vice President, Sales	1970-02-19
Steven	Buchanan	Sales Manager	1973-03-04
Laura	Callahan	Inside Sales Coordinator	1976-01-09
Robert	King	Sales Representative	1978-05-29
Michael	Suyama	Sales Representative	1981-07-02
Janet	Leverling	Sales Representative	1981-08-30
Anne	Dodsworth	Sales Representative	1984-01-27

Hint

Use the Convert function to convert the BirthDate column (originally a DateTime column) to a Date column.

12. Employees full name

Show the FirstName and LastName columns from the Employees table, and then create a new column called FullName, showing FirstName and LastName joined together in one column, with a space in-between.

Expected Results

FirstName	LastName	FullName
Nancy	Davolio	Nancy Davolio
Andrew	Fuller	Andrew Fuller
Janet	Leverling	Janet Leverling
Margaret	Peacock	Margaret Peacock
Steven	Buchanan	Steven Buchanan
Michael	Suyama	Michael Suyama
Robert	King	Robert King
Laura	Callahan	Laura Callahan
Anne	Dodsworth	Anne Dodsworth

Joining two fields like this is called concatenation. Look online for examples of string concatenation with SQL Server.

13. OrderDetails amount per line item

In the OrderDetails table, we have the fields UnitPrice and Quantity. Create a new field, TotalPrice, that multiplies these two together. We'll ignore the Discount field for now.

In addition, show the OrderID, ProductID, UnitPrice, and Quantity. Order by OrderID and ProductID.

Expected Results

OrderID	ProductID	UnitPrice	Quantity	TotalPrice
10248	11	14.00	12	168.00
10248	42	9.80	10	98.00
10248	72	34.80	5	174.00
10249	14	18.60	9	167.40
10249	51	42.40	40	1696.00
10250	41	7.70	10	77.00
10250	51	42.40	35	1484.00
10250	65	16.80	15	252.00
10251	22	16.80	6	100.80
10251	57	15.60	15	234.00
10251	65	16.80	20	336.00
10252	20	64.80	40	2592.00
10252	33	2.00	25	50.00
10252	60	27.20	40	1088.00
10253	31	10.00	20	200.00
10253	39	14.40	42	604.80
10253	49	16.00	40	640.00
10254	24	3.60	15	54.00
10254	55	19.20	21	403.20
10254	74	8.00	21	168.00
10255	2	15.20	20	304.00
10255	16	13.90	35	486.50

(Some rows were not included, the total should be 2155)

Hint

In this computed column, you need to use the arithmetic operator for multiplication.

14.   How many customers?

How many customers do we have in the Customers table? Show one value only, and don't rely on getting the record count at the end of a resultset.

Expected Results

TotalCustomers
91

Hint

In order to get the total number of customers, we need to use what's called an aggregate function. Look online for an aggregate function that would work for this problem.

15.   When was the first order?

Show the date of the first order ever made in the Orders table.

Expected Results

FirstOrder
2014-07-04 08:00:00.000

Hint

There's an aggregate function called Min that you will need for this problem.

16. Countries where there are customers

Show a list of countries where the Northwind company has customers.

Country
Argentina
Austria
Belgium
Brazil
Canada
Denmark
Finland
France
Germany
Ireland
Italy
Mexico
Norway
Poland
Portugal
Spain
Sweden
Switzerland
UK
USA
Venezuela

Hint

You'll want to use the Group By clause for this query.

17. Contact titles for customers

Show a list of all the different values in the Customers table for ContactTitles. Also include a count for each ContactTitle.

This is similar in concept to the previous question "Countries where there are customers", except we now want a count for each ContactTitle.

ContactTitle	TotalContactTitle
Owner	17
Sales Representative	17
Marketing Manager	12
Sales Manager	11
Accounting Manager	10
Sales Associate	7
Marketing Assistant	6
Sales Agent	5
Assistant Sales Agent	2
Order Administrator	2
Assistant Sales Representative	1
Owner/Marketing Assistant	1

Hint

The answer for this problem builds on multiple concepts introduced in previous problems, such as grouping, aggregate functions, and aliases.

18. Products with associated supplier names

We'd like to show, for each product, the associated Supplier. Show the ProductID, ProductName, and the CompanyName of the Supplier.

Sort the result by ProductID.

This question will introduce what may be a new concept—the Join clause in SQL. The Join clause is used to join two or more relational database tables together in a logical way. In this case, you will join the Suppliers table to the Products table by SupplierID.

Expected Results

ProductID	ProductName	Supplier

1	Chai	Exotic Liquids
2	Chang	Exotic Liquids
3	Aniseed Syrup	Exotic Liquids
4	Chef Anton's Cajun Seasoning	New Orleans Cajun Delights
5	Chef Anton's Gumbo Mix	New Orleans Cajun Delights
6	Grandma's Boysenberry Spread	Grandma Kelly's Homestead
7	Uncle Bob's Organic Dried Pears	Grandma Kelly's Homestead
8	Northwoods Cranberry Sauce	Grandma Kelly's Homestead
9	Mishi Kobe Niku	Tokyo Traders
10	Ikura	Tokyo Traders
11	Queso Cabrales	Cooperativa de Quesos 'Las Cabras'
12	Queso Manchego La Pastora	Cooperativa de Quesos 'Las Cabras'
13	Konbu	Mayumi's
14	Tofu	Mayumi's
15	Genen Shouyu	Mayumi's
16	Pavlova	Pavlova, Ltd.
17	Alice Mutton	Pavlova, Ltd.
18	Carnarvon Tigers	Pavlova, Ltd.
19	Teatime Chocolate Biscuits	Specialty Biscuits, Ltd.
20	Sir Rodney's Marmalade	Specialty Biscuits, Ltd.
21	Sir Rodney's Scones	Specialty Biscuits, Ltd.

(Some rows were not included, the total should be 77)

Hint

Just as a reference, here's an example of what the syntax for the Join looks like, using different tables from the Northwind database. It will show all the products, with the associated CategoryName.

```
Select
    ProductID
    ,ProductName
    ,CategoryName
From Products
    Join Categories
        on Products.CategoryID = Categories.CategoryID
```

19.   Orders and the Shipper that was used

We'd like to show a list of the Orders that were made, including the Shipper that was used. Show the OrderID, OrderDate (date only), and CompanyName of the Shipper, and sort by OrderID.

In order to not show all the orders (there's more than 800), show only those rows with an OrderID of less than 10270.

Expected Results

OrderID	OrderDate	Shipper
10248	2014-07-04	Federal Shipping
10249	2014-07-05	Speedy Express
10250	2014-07-08	United Package
10251	2014-07-08	Speedy Express
10252	2014-07-09	United Package
10253	2014-07-10	United Package
10254	2014-07-11	United Package
10255	2014-07-12	Federal Shipping
10256	2014-07-15	United Package
10257	2014-07-16	Federal Shipping
10258	2014-07-17	Speedy Express
10259	2014-07-18	Federal Shipping
10260	2014-07-19	Speedy Express
10261	2014-07-19	United Package
10262	2014-07-22	Federal Shipping
10263	2014-07-23	Federal Shipping
10264	2014-07-24	Federal Shipping
10265	2014-07-25	Speedy Express
10266	2014-07-26	Federal Shipping
10267	2014-07-29	Speedy Express
10268	2014-07-30	Federal Shipping
10269	2014-07-31	Speedy Express

Hint

First, create a SQL statement that shows only the rows and columns you need from the Orders table. Then, work on adding the join to the Shipper table, and the necessary field from that table. You should be able to look at the Orders table to figure out the field to use for the join.

Something to note for this problem is that when you join two tables, the field that's joined on does not necessarily need to have the same name. Usually, they do. However, in this case, the ShipVia field in Orders is joined to ShipperID in Shippers.

Congratulations! You've completed the introductory problems.

Enjoying this book so far? I'd love for you to share your thoughts and post a quick review on Amazon!

Any feedback on the problems, hints, or answers? I'd like to hear from you. Please email me at feedback@SQLPracticeProblems.com.

Intermediate Problems

20.   Categories, and the total products in each category

For this problem, we'd like to see the total number of products in each category. Sort the results by the total number of products, in descending order.

Expected Results

CategoryName	TotalProducts
Confections	13
Beverages	12
Condiments	12
Seafood	12
Dairy Products	10
Grains/Cereals	7
Meat/Poultry	6
Produce	5

Hint

To solve this problem, you need to combine a join, and a group by.

A good way to start is by creating a query that shows the CategoryName and all ProductIDs associated with it, without grouping. Then, add the Group by.

21.   Total customers per country/city

In the Customers table, show the total number of customers per Country and City.

Expected Results

Country	City	TotalCustomers
UK	London	6
Mexico	México D.F.	5
Brazil	Sao Paulo	4

Brazil	Rio de Janeiro	3
Spain	Madrid	3
Argentina	Buenos Aires	3
France	Paris	2
USA	Portland	2
France	Nantes	2
Portugal	Lisboa	2
Finland	Oulu	1
Italy	Reggio Emilia	1
France	Reims	1
Brazil	Resende	1
Austria	Salzburg	1
Venezuela	San Cristóbal	1
USA	San Francisco	1
USA	Seattle	1

(Some rows were not included, the total should be 69)

Hint

Just as you can have multiple fields in a Select clause, you can also have multiple fields in a Group By clause.

22.   Products that need reordering

What products do we have in our inventory that should be reordered? For now, just use the fields UnitsInStock and ReorderLevel, where UnitsInStock is less than or equal to the ReorderLevel, Ignore the fields UnitsOnOrder and Discontinued.

Sort the results by ProductID.

Expected Results

ProductID	ProductName	UnitsInStock	ReorderLevel
2	Chang	17	25
3	Aniseed Syrup	13	25
5	Chef Anton's Gumbo Mix	0	0
11	Queso Cabrales	22	30

17	Alice Mutton	0	0
21	Sir Rodney's Scones	3	5
29	Thüringer Rostbratwurst	0	0
30	Nord-Ost Matjeshering	10	15
31	Gorgonzola Telino	0	20
32	Mascarpone Fabioli	9	25
37	Gravad lax	11	25
43	Ipoh Coffee	17	25
45	Rogede sild	5	15
48	Chocolade	15	25
49	Maxilaku	10	15
53	Perth Pasties	0	0
56	Gnocchi di nonna Alice	21	30
64	Wimmers gute Semmelknödel	22	30
66	Louisiana Hot Spiced Okra	4	20
68	Scottish Longbreads	6	15
70	Outback Lager	15	30
74	Longlife Tofu	4	5

Hint

We want to show all fields where the UnitsInStock is less than or equal to the ReorderLevel. So, in the Where clause, use the following:

```
UnitsInStock <= ReorderLevel
```

23.   Products that need reordering, continued

Now we need to incorporate these fields—UnitsInStock, UnitsOnOrder, ReorderLevel, Discontinued—into our calculation. We'll define "products that need reordering" with the following:

- UnitsInStock plus UnitsOnOrder are less than or equal to ReorderLevel
- The Discontinued flag is false (0).

Expected Results

Product ID	Product Name	Units In Stock	Units On Order	Reorder Level	Discontinued

| 30 | Nord-Ost Matjeshering | 10 | 0 | 15 | 0 |
| 70 | Outback Lager | 15 | 10 | 30 | 0 |

Hint

For the first part of the Where clause, you should have something like this:

```
UnitsInStock + UnitsOnOrder <= ReorderLevel
```

24. Customer list by region

A salesperson for Northwind is going on a business trip to visit customers, and would like to see a list of all customers, sorted by region, alphabetically.

However, he wants the customers with no region (null in the Region field) to be at the end, instead of at the top, where you'd normally find the null values. Within the same region, companies should be sorted by CustomerID.

Expected Results

CustomerID	CompanyName	Region
OLDWO	Old World Delicatessen	AK
BOTTM	Bottom-Dollar Markets	BC
LAUGB	Laughing Bacchus Wine Cellars	BC
LETSS	Let's Stop N Shop	CA
HUNGO	Hungry Owl All-Night Grocers	Co. Cork
GROSR	GROSELLA-Restaurante	DF
SAVEA	Save-a-lot Markets	ID
ISLAT	Island Trading	Isle of Wight
LILAS	LILA-Supermercado	Lara
THECR	The Cracker Box	MT
RATTC	Rattlesnake Canyon Grocery	NM
LINOD	LINO-Delicateses	Nueva Esparta
GREAL	Great Lakes Food Market	OR
HUNGC	Hungry Coyote Import Store	OR
	(skipping some rows in the middle, the total rows returned should be 91)	

TORTU	Tortuga Restaurante	NULL
VAFFE	Vaffeljernet	NULL
VICTE	Victuailles en stock	NULL
VINET	Vins et alcools Chevalier	NULL
WANDK	Die Wandernde Kuh	NULL
WARTH	Wartian Herkku	NULL
WILMK	Wilman Kala	NULL
WOLZA	Wolski Zajazd	NULL

Hint

You won't be able to sort directly on the Region field here. You'll need to sort on the Region field, and also on a computed field that you create, which will give you a secondary sort for when Region is null

First, without ordering, create a computed field with a value that will sort the way you want. In this case, you can create a field with the Case statement. This allows you to do if/then logic. You want a field that is 1 when Region is null.

Take a look at the Examples section in the SQL Server documentation for the Case statement (https://docs.microsoft.com/en-us/sql/t-sql/language-elements/case-transact-sql?view=sql-server-2017#examples).

Note that when filtering for null values, you can't use "FieldName = Null". You must use "FieldName is null".

Hint

You should have something like this:

```
Select
    CustomerID
    ,CompanyName
    ,Region
    ,Case
        when Region is null then 1
        else 0
    End
From Customers
```

When the Region contains a null, you will have a 1 in the final column. Now, just add the fields for the Order By clause, in the right order.

25. High freight charges

Some of the countries we ship to have very high freight charges. We'd like to investigate some more shipping options for our customers, to be able to offer them lower freight charges. Return the three ship countries with the highest average freight overall, in descending order by average freight.

Expected Results

ShipCountry	AverageFreight
Austria	184.7875
Ireland	145.0126
USA	112.8794

Hint

We'll be using the Orders table, and using the Freight and ShipCountry fields.

Hint

You'll want to group by ShipCountry, and use the Avg function. Don't worry about showing only the top 3 rows until you have the grouping and average freight set up.

Hint

You should have something like this:

```
Select
    ShipCountry
    ,AverageFreight = avg(freight)
From Orders
Group By ShipCountry
Order By AverageFreight desc
```

Now you just need to show just the top 3 rows.

26.   High freight charges—2015

We're continuing on the question above on high freight charges. Now, instead of using *all* the orders we have, we only want to see orders from the year 2015.

Expected result

ShipCountry	AverageFreight
Austria	178.3642
Switzerland	117.1775
France	113.991

Hint

You need to add a Where clause to the query from the previous problem. The field to filter on is OrderDate.

Hint

When filtering on dates, you need to know whether the date field is a DateTime, or a Date field. Is OrderDate a Datetime or a Date field?

27.   High freight charges with between

Another (incorrect) answer to the problem above is this:

```
Select Top 3
    ShipCountry
    ,AverageFreight = avg(freight)
From Orders
Where
    OrderDate between '20150101' and '20151231'
Group By ShipCountry
Order By AverageFreight desc
```

Notice when you run this, it shows Sweden as the ShipCountry with the third highest freight charges. However, this is wrong—it should be France.

What is the OrderID of the order that the (incorrect) answer above is missing?

(no expected results this time—we're looking for one specific OrderID)

Hint

The Between statement is inclusive. Why isn't it showing the orders made on December 31, 2015?

Hint

Run this query, and look at the rows around December 31, 2015. What do you notice? Look specifically at the Freight field.

```
select * from orders order by OrderDate
```

28.   High freight charges—last year

We're continuing to work on high freight charges. We now want to get the three ship countries with the highest average freight charges. But instead of filtering for a particular year, we want to use the last 12 months of order data, using as the end date the last OrderDate in Orders.

Expected Results

ShipCountry	AverageFreight
Ireland	200.21
Austria	186.4596
USA	119.3032

Hint

First, get the last OrderDate in Orders. Write a simple select statement to get the highest value in the OrderDate field using the Max aggregate function.

You should have something like this:

```
Select Max(OrderDate) from Orders
```

Now you need to get the date 1 year before the last order date. Create a simple select statement that subtracts 1 year from the last order date

You can use the DateAdd function for this. Note that within DateAdd, you can use the subquery you created above. Look online for some examples if you need to.

You should have something like this:

```
Select Dateadd(yy, -1, (Select Max(OrderDate) from Orders))
```

Now you just need to put it in the where clause.

29.   Employee/Order Detail report

We're doing inventory, and need to show Employee and Order Detail information like the below, for all orders. Sort by OrderID and Product ID.

Expected Results

EmployeeID	LastName	OrderID	ProductName	Quantity
5	Buchanan	10248	Queso Cabrales	12
5	Buchanan	10248	Singaporean Hokkien Fried Mee	10
5	Buchanan	10248	Mozzarella di Giovanni	5
6	Suyama	10249	Tofu	9
6	Suyama	10249	Manjimup Dried Apples	40
4	Peacock	10250	Jack's New England Clam Chowder	10
4	Peacock	10250	Manjimup Dried Apples	35
4	Peacock	10250	Louisiana Fiery Hot Pepper Sauce	15
3	Leverling	10251	Gustaf's Knäckebröd	6
3	Leverling	10251	Ravioli Angelo	15
3	Leverling	10251	Louisiana Fiery Hot Pepper Sauce	20
4	Peacock	10252	Sir Rodney's Marmalade	40

4	Peacock	10252	Geitost	25
4	Peacock	10252	Camembert Pierrot	40
3	Leverling	10253	Gorgonzola Telino	20
3	Leverling	10253	Chartreuse verte	42
3	Leverling	10253	Maxilaku	40
5	Buchanan	10254	Guaraná Fantástica	15
5	Buchanan	10254	Pâté chinois	21
5	Buchanan	10254	Longlife Tofu	21

(Some rows were not included, the total should be 2155)

Hint

You'll need to do a join between 4 tables, displaying only those fields that are necessary.

30. Customers with no orders

There are some customers who have never actually placed an order. Show these customers.

Expected Results

Customers_CustomerID	Orders_CustomerID
FISSA	NULL
PARIS	NULL

Hint

One way of doing this is to use a left join, also known as a left outer join.

Hint

```
Select
    Customers_CustomerID = Customers.CustomerID
    ,Orders_CustomerID = Orders.CustomerID
From Customers
    left join Orders
```

```
on Orders.CustomerID = Customers.CustomerID
```

This is a good start. It shows all records from the Customers table, and the matching records from the Orders table. However, we only want those records where the CustomerID in Orders is null. You still need a filter

31.   Customers with no orders for EmployeeID 4

One employee (Margaret Peacock, EmployeeID 4) has placed the most orders. However, there are some customers who've never placed an order with her. Show only those customers who have never placed an order with her.

Expected Result

CustomerID	CustomerID
CONSH	NULL
DUMON	NULL
FISSA	NULL
FRANR	NULL
GROSR	NULL
LAUGB	NULL
LAZYK	NULL
NORTS	NULL
PARIS	NULL
PERIC	NULL
PRINI	NULL
SANTG	NULL
SEVES	NULL
SPECD	NULL
THEBI	NULL
VINET	NULL

Hint

Building on the previous problem, you might (incorrectly) think you need to do something like this:

```
Select
    Customers.CustomerID
    ,Orders.CustomerID
From Customers
    left join Orders
        on Orders.CustomerID = Customers.CustomerID
Where
    Orders.CustomerID is null
    and Orders.EmployeeID = 4
```

Notice that this filter was added in the where clause:

`and Orders.EmployeeID = 4`

However, this returns no records.

With outer joins, the filters on the where clause are applied *after* the join.

Congratulations! You've completed the intermediate problems.

Enjoying this book so far? I'd love for you to share your thoughts and post a quick review on Amazon!

Any feedback on the problems, hints, or answers? I'd like to hear from you. Please email me at feedback@SQLPracticeProblems.com.

Advanced Problems

32. High-value customers

We want to send all of our high-value customers a special VIP gift. We're defining high-value customers as those who've made at least 1 order with a total value (not including the discount) equal to $10,000 or more. We only want to consider orders made in the year 2016.

Expected Result

CustomerID	CompanyName	OrderID	TotalOrderAmount
QUICK	QUICK-Stop	10865	17250.00
SAVEA	Save-a-lot Markets	11030	16321.90
HANAR	Hanari Carnes	10981	15810.00
KOENE	Königlich Essen	10817	11490.70
RATTC	Rattlesnake Canyon Grocery	10889	11380.00
HUNGO	Hungry Owl All-Night Grocers	10897	10835.24

Hint

First, let's get the necessary fields for all orders made in the year 2016. Don't bother grouping yet, just work on the Where clause. You'll need the CustomerID, CompanyName from Customers; OrderID from Orders; and Quantity and unit price from OrderDetails. Order by the total amount of the order, in descending order.

Hint

You should have something like this:

```
Select
    Customers.CustomerID
    ,Customers.CompanyName
```

```
        ,Orders.OrderID
        ,Amount = Quantity * UnitPrice
From Customers
    join Orders
        on Orders.CustomerID = Customers.CustomerID
    join OrderDetails
        on Orders.OrderID = OrderDetails.OrderID
Where
    OrderDate >= '20160101'
    and OrderDate  < '20170101'
```

This gives you the total amount for each Order Detail item in 2016 orders, at the Order Detail level. Now, which fields do you need to group on, and which need to be summed?

Hint

```
Select
    Customers.CustomerID
    ,Customers.CompanyName
    ,Orders.OrderID
    ,TotalOrderAmount = sum(Quantity * UnitPrice)
From Customers
    Join Orders
        on Orders.CustomerID = Customers.CustomerID
    Join OrderDetails
        on Orders.OrderID = OrderDetails.OrderID
Where
    OrderDate >= '20160101'
    and OrderDate  < '20170101'
Group By
    Customers.CustomerID
    ,Customers.CompanyName
    ,Orders.OrderID
```

The fields at the Customer and Order level need to be grouped by, and the TotalOrderAmount needs to be summed.

How would you filter on the sum, in order to get orders of $10,000 or more? Can you put it straight into the where clause?

33. High-value customers—total orders

The manager has changed his mind. Instead of requiring that customers have at least one individual order totaling $10,000 or more, he wants to define high-value customers differently. Now, high value customers are customers who have orders totaling $15,000 or more in 2016. How would you change the answer to the problem above?

Expected Result

CustomerID	CompanyName	TotalOrderAmount
SAVEA	Save-a-lot Markets	42806.25
ERNSH	Ernst Handel	42598.90
QUICK	QUICK-Stop	40526.99
HANAR	Hanari Carnes	24238.05
HUNGO	Hungry Owl All-Night Grocers	22796.34
RATTC	Rattlesnake Canyon Grocery	21725.60
KOENE	Königlich Essen	20204.95
FOLKO	Folk och fä HB	15973.85
WHITC	White Clover Markets	15278.90

Hint

This query is almost identical to the one above, but there's just a few lines you need to delete or comment out, to group at a different level.

34. High-value customers—with discount

Change the answer from the previous problem to use the discount when calculating high-value customers. Order by the total amount, taking into consideration the discount.

Expected Result

Customer ID	Company Name	Totals Without Discount	Totals With Discount
ERNSH	Ernst Handel	42598.90	41210.6500244141
QUICK	QUICK-Stop	40526.99	37217.3150024414
SAVEA	Save-a-lot Markets	42806.25	36310.1097793579

HANAR	Hanari Carnes	24238.05	23821.1999893188
RATTC	Rattlesnake Canyon Grocery	21725.60	21238.2704410553
HUNGO	Hungry Owl All-Night Grocers	22796.34	20402.119934082
KOENE	Königlich Essen	20204.95	19582.7739868164
WHITC	White Clover Markets	15278.90	15278.8999862671

Hint

To start out, just use the OrderDetails table. You'll need to figure out how the Discount field is structured.

Hint

You should have something like this:

```
Select
    OrderID
    ,ProductID
    ,UnitPrice
    ,Quantity
    ,Discount
    ,TotalWithDisccount = UnitPrice * Quantity * (1- Discount)
from OrderDetails
```

Note that Discount is applied as a percentage. So, if there's a 0.15 in the discount field, you need to multiply the UnitPrice * Quantity by .85 (1.00 - .15). You need parenthesis around (1 - Discount) to make sure that calculation is done first.

35.   Month-end orders

At the end of the month, salespeople are likely to try much harder to get orders, to meet their month-end quotas. Show all orders made on the last day of the month. Order by EmployeeID and OrderID

Expected Result

EmployeeID	OrderID	OrderDate
1	10461	2015-02-28 00:00:00.000
1	10616	2015-07-31 00:00:00.000
2	10583	2015-06-30 00:00:00.000
2	10686	2015-09-30 00:00:00.000
2	10989	2016-03-31 00:00:00.000
2	11060	2016-04-30 00:00:00.000
3	10432	2015-01-31 00:00:00.000
3	10988	2016-03-31 00:00:00.000
3	11063	2016-04-30 00:00:00.000
4	10343	2014-10-31 00:00:00.000
4	10522	2015-04-30 00:00:00.000
4	10584	2015-06-30 00:00:00.000
4	10617	2015-07-31 00:00:00.000
4	10725	2015-10-31 00:00:00.000
4	11061	2016-04-30 00:00:00.000
4	11062	2016-04-30 00:00:00.000
5	10269	2014-07-31 00:00:00.000
6	10317	2014-09-30 00:00:00.000
7	10490	2015-03-31 00:00:00.000
8	10399	2014-12-31 00:00:00.000
8	10460	2015-02-28 00:00:00.000
8	10491	2015-03-31 00:00:00.000
8	10987	2016-03-31 00:00:00.000
9	10687	2015-09-30 00:00:00.000

Hint

You can work on developing the end of month calculation yourself, with a combination of date functions such as DateAdd and DateDiff. But feel free to shortcut the process by doing some research online.

36. Orders with many line items

The Northwind mobile app developers are testing an app that customers will use to show orders. In order to make sure that even the largest orders will show up correctly on the app, they'd like some samples of orders that have lots of individual line items.

Show the 10 orders with the most line items, in order of total line items.

Expected Result

OrderID	TotalOrderDetails
11077	25
10657	6
10847	6
10979	6
10273	5
10294	5
10309	5
10324	5
10325	5
10337	5

Hint

Using the OrderDetails table, you'll use Group by and Count().

37.   Orders—random assortment

The Northwind mobile app developers would now like to just get a random assortment of orders for beta testing on their app. Show a random set of 2% of all orders.

(Note—your results will be different, because we're returning a random set. However, there should be 17 rows returned)

OrderID
10860
11060
10350
10526
10624
10688
10781
10929
10540
11041
10758
10599
10248
10660
10298
10783
10302

Hint

Note that in the below SQL, the RandomValue field returns the *same* random value for each row. Do some research online to figure out how to get a *new* random value for each row.

```
Select
    OrderID
    , RandomValue = Rand()
From Orders
```

38. Orders—accidental double-entry

One of the salespeople has come to you with a request. She thinks that she accidentally entered a line item twice on an order, each time with a different ProductID, but the exact same quantity. She remembers that the quantity was 60 or more. Show all the OrderIDs with line items that match this, in order of OrderID.

Expected Result

OrderID
10263
10263
10658
10990
11030

Hint

You might start out with something like this:

```
Select
    OrderID
    ,ProductID
    ,Quantity
From OrderDetails
Where Quantity >= 60
```

However, this will only give us the orders where at least one order detail has a quantity of 60 or more. We need to show orders with *more* than one order detail with a quantity of 60 or more. Also, the same value for quantity needs to be there more than once.

Hint

In addition to grouping on the OrderID, we also need to group by the Quantity, since we need to show the order details that have the same quantity, within an order. So, we need to group by both OrderID, and Quantity.

39. Orders—accidental double-entry details

Based on the previous question, we now want to show details of the order, for orders that match the above criteria.

Expected Result

OrderID	ProductID	UnitPrice	Quantity	Discount
10263	16	13.90	60	0.25
10263	30	20.70	60	0.25
10263	24	3.60	65	0
10263	74	8.00	65	0.25
10658	60	34.00	55	0.05
10658	21	10.00	60	0
10658	40	18.40	70	0.05
10658	77	13.00	70	0.05
10990	34	14.00	60	0.15
10990	21	10.00	65	0
10990	55	24.00	65	0.15
10990	61	28.50	66	0.15
11030	29	123.79	60	0.25
11030	5	21.35	70	0
11030	2	19.00	100	0.25
11030	59	55.00	100	0.25

Hint

There are many ways of doing this, including CTE (common table expression) and derived tables. I suggest using a CTE and a subquery. You can see some CTE examples here: https://docs.microsoft.com/en-us/sql/t-sql/queries/with-common-table-expression-transact-sql?#examples. Or, search online for "SQL common table expression examples"

This is an example of a simple CTE in Northwind. It returns orders made by the oldest employee:

```
;with OldestEmployee as (
    Select top 1
        EmployeeID
    from Employees
    order by BirthDate
)
Select
```

```
OrderID
    ,OrderDate
from Orders
where
    EmployeeID in (Select EmployeeID from OldestEmployee)
```

40.   Orders—accidental double-entry details, derived table

Here's another way of getting the same results as in the previous problem, using a derived table instead of a CTE. However, there's a bug in this SQL. It returns 20 rows instead of 16. Correct the SQL.

Problem SQL:

```
Select
    OrderDetails.OrderID
    ,ProductID
    ,UnitPrice
    ,Quantity
    ,Discount
From OrderDetails
    Join (
        Select
            OrderID
        From OrderDetails
        Where Quantity >= 60
        Group By OrderID, Quantity
        Having Count(*) > 1
    ) PotentialProblemOrders
        on PotentialProblemOrders.OrderID = OrderDetails.OrderID
Order by OrderID, ProductID
```

Hint

Your first step should be to run the SQL in the derived table

```
Select
    OrderID
From OrderDetails
Where Quantity >= 60
Group By OrderID, Quantity
```

```
Having Count(*) > 1
```

What do you notice about the results?

Hint

There are 2 rows for OrderID 10263, because there are 2 sets of rows that have the same, identical quantity, that's 60 or above.

When you do a join to a table that has duplicates, you will get duplicates in the output as well, unless you take steps to avoid it.

Find a single keyword that you can easily add to avoid duplicates in SQL.

41.   Late orders

Some customers are complaining about their orders arriving late. Which orders are late? Sort the results by OrderID.

Expected Result

OrderID	OrderDate	RequiredDate	ShippedDate
10264	2014-07-24	2014-08-21	2014-08-23
10271	2014-08-01	2014-08-29	2014-08-30
10280	2014-08-14	2014-09-11	2014-09-12
10302	2014-09-10	2014-10-08	2014-10-09
10309	2014-09-19	2014-10-17	2014-10-23
10380	2014-12-12	2015-01-09	2015-01-16
10423	2015-01-23	2015-02-06	2015-02-24
10427	2015-01-27	2015-02-24	2015-03-03
10433	2015-02-03	2015-03-03	2015-03-04
10451	2015-02-19	2015-03-05	2015-03-12
10483	2015-03-24	2015-04-21	2015-04-25
10515	2015-04-23	2015-05-07	2015-05-23
10523	2015-05-01	2015-05-29	2015-05-30
10545	2015-05-22	2015-06-19	2015-06-26
10578	2015-06-24	2015-07-22	2015-07-25
10593	2015-07-09	2015-08-06	2015-08-13
10596	2015-07-11	2015-08-08	2015-08-12

| 10660 | 2015-09-08 | 2015-10-06 | 2015-10-15 |

(Some rows were not included, your total should be 39)

Hint

To determine which orders are late, you can use a combination of the RequiredDate and ShippedDate. It's not exact, but if ShippedDate is actually *after* RequiredDate, you can be sure it's late.

42. Late orders—which employees?

Some salespeople have more orders arriving late than others. Maybe they're not following up on the order process, and need more training. Which salespeople have the most orders arriving late?

Expected Result

EmployeeID	LastName	TotalLateOrders
4	Peacock	10
3	Leverling	5
8	Callahan	5
9	Dodsworth	5
7	King	4
2	Fuller	4
1	Davolio	3
6	Suyama	3

Hint

The answer from the earlier problem, "Late Orders", is a good starting point. You'll need to join to the Employee table to get the last name, and also add Count to show the total late orders.

43.   Late orders vs. total orders

Andrew, the VP of sales, has been doing some more thinking some more about the problem of late orders. He realizes that just looking at the number of orders arriving late for each salesperson isn't a good idea. It needs to be compared to the *total* number of orders per salesperson. We want results like the following:

Expected Result

EmployeeID	LastName	AllOrders	LateOrders
1	Davolio	123	3
2	Fuller	96	4
3	Leverling	127	5
4	Peacock	156	10
6	Suyama	67	3
7	King	72	4
8	Callahan	104	5
9	Dodsworth	43	5

Hint

You can use more than one CTE in a query. That would be a straightforward way of solving this problem.

Hint

Here are 2 SQL statements that could be put into CTEs and put together into a final SQL statement.

```
-- Late orders
Select
    EmployeeID
    ,TotalOrders = Count(*)
From Orders
Where
    RequiredDate <= ShippedDate
Group By
    EmployeeID

-- Total orders
Select
```

```
    EmployeeID
    ,TotalOrders = Count(*)
From Orders
Group By
    EmployeeID
```

44.   Late orders vs. total orders—missing employee

There's an employee missing in the answer from the problem above. Fix the SQL to show all employees who have taken orders.

Expected Result

EmployeeID	LastName	AllOrders	LateOrders
1	Davolio	123	3
2	Fuller	96	4
3	Leverling	127	5
4	Peacock	156	10
5	Buchanan	42	NULL
6	Suyama	67	3
7	King	72	4
8	Callahan	104	5
9	Dodsworth	43	5

Hint

How many rows are returned when you run just the AllOrders CTE? How about when you run just the LateOrders CTE?

Hint

You'll want to add a left join (also known as a left outer join), to make sure that we show a row, even if there are no late orders.

45.   Late orders vs. total orders—fix null

Continuing on the answer for the previous problem, let's fix the results for row 5 - Buchanan. He should have a 0 instead of a Null in LateOrders.

Expected Result

EmployeeID	LastName	AllOrders	LateOrders
1	Davolio	123	3
2	Fuller	96	4
3	Leverling	127	5
4	Peacock	156	10
5	Buchanan	42	0
6	Suyama	67	3
7	King	72	4
8	Callahan	104	5
9	Dodsworth	43	5

Hint

Find a function to test if a value is null, and return a different value when it is.

46.   Late orders vs. total orders—percentage

Now we want to get the percentage of late orders over total orders.

Expected Result

Employee ID	Last Name	All Orders	Late Orders	Percent Late Orders
1	Davolio	123	3	0.0243902439024
2	Fuller	96	4	0.0416666666666
3	Leverling	127	5	0.0393700787401
4	Peacock	156	10	0.0641025641025
5	Buchanan	42	0	0.0000000000000
6	Suyama	67	3	0.0447761194029
7	King	72	4	0.0555555555555
8	Callahan	104	5	0.0480769230769

9	Dodsworth	43	5	0.1162790697674

Hint

By dividing late orders by total orders, you should be able to get the percentage of orders that are late. However, there's a common problem people run into, which is that an integer divided by an integer returns an integer. For instance, if you run the following SQL to divide 3 by 2:

```
select 3/2
```

You'll get 1 instead of 1.5, because it will return the closest integer.

Do some research online to find the answer to this issue.

47. Late orders vs. total orders—fix decimal

So now for the PercentageLateOrders, we get a decimal value like we should. But to make the output easier to read, let's cut the PercentLateOrders off at 2 digits to the right of the decimal point.

Expected Result

Employee ID	Last Name	All Orders	Late Orders	Percent Late Orders
1	Davolio	123	3	0.02
2	Fuller	96	4	0.04
3	Leverling	127	5	0.04
4	Peacock	156	10	0.06
5	Buchanan	42	0	0.00
6	Suyama	67	3	0.04
7	King	72	4	0.06
8	Callahan	104	5	0.05
9	Dodsworth	43	5	0.12

One straightforward way of doing this would be to explicitly convert PercentageLateOrders to a specific Decimal data type. With the Decimal datatype, you can specify how many digits you want to the right of the decimal point.

The calculation PercentLateOrders is getting a little long and complicated, and it can be tricky to get all the commas and parenthesis correct.

As you're working on it, one way to simplify it is to break it down with an actual value instead of a calculation.

For instance:

```
Select convert(decimal(2,2), 0.0243902439024)
```

48.   Customer grouping

Andrew Fuller, the VP of sales at Northwind, would like to do a sales campaign for existing customers. He'd like to categorize customers into groups, based on how much they ordered in 2016. Then, depending on which group the customer is in, he will target the customer with different sales materials.

The customer grouping categories are 0 to 1,000, 1,000 to 5,000, 5,000 to 10,000, and over 10,000. So, if the total dollar amount of the customer's purchases in that year were between 0 to 1,000, they would be in the "Low" group. A customer with purchase from 1,000 to 5,000 would be in the "Medium" group, and so on.

A good starting point for this query is the answer from the problem "High-value customers—total orders". Also, we only want to show customers who have ordered in 2016.

Order the results by CustomerID.

Expected Result

CustomerID	Company Name	Total Order Amount	Customer Group

ALFKI	Alfreds Futterkiste	2302.20	Medium
ANATR	Ana Trujillo Emparedados y helados	514.40	Low
ANTON	Antonio Moreno Taquería	660.00	Low
AROUT	Around the Horn	5838.50	High
BERGS	Berglunds snabbköp	8110.55	High
BLAUS	Blauer See Delikatessen	2160.00	Medium
BLONP	Blondesddsl père et fils	730.00	Low
BOLID	Bólido Comidas preparadas	280.00	Low
BONAP	Bon app'	7185.90	High
BOTTM	Bottom-Dollar Markets	12227.40	Very High
BSBEV	B's Beverages	2431.00	Medium
CACTU	Cactus Comidas para llevar	1576.80	Medium
CHOPS	Chop-suey Chinese	4429.40	Medium
COMMI	Comércio Mineiro	513.75	Low
CONSH	Consolidated Holdings	931.50	Low
DRACD	Drachenblut Delikatessen	2809.61	Medium
DUMON	Du monde entier	860.10	Low
EASTC	Eastern Connection	9569.31	High
ERNSH	Ernst Handel	42598.90	Very High
FOLKO	Folk och fä HB	15973.85	Very High
FRANK	Frankenversand	5587.00	High

(Some rows were not included, the total should be 81)

Hint

This is the SQL from the problem "High-value customers—total orders", but without the filter for order totals over 10,000.

```
Select
    Customers.CustomerID
    ,Customers.CompanyName
    ,TotalOrderAmount = SUM(Quantity * UnitPrice)
From Customers
    Join Orders
        on Orders.CustomerID = Customers.CustomerID
    Join OrderDetails
        on Orders.OrderID = OrderDetails.OrderID
Where
    OrderDate >= '20160101'
```

```
    and OrderDate  < '20170101'
Group By
    Customers.CustomerID
    ,Customers.CompanyName
Order By TotalOrderAmount Desc
```

Hint

You can use the above SQL in a CTE (common table expression), and then build on it, using a Case statement on the TotalOrderAmount.

49. Customer grouping—fix null

There's a problem with the answer to the previous question. The CustomerGroup value for one of the rows is null.

Fix the SQL so that there are no nulls in the CustomerGroup field.

Expected Result

CustomerID	Company Name	Total Order Amount	Customer Group
MAISD	Maison Dewey	5000.20	High

(The total output is still 81 rows, but here we're only showing the row which had a null CustomerGroup value in the answer to the previous problem.)

Hint

What is the total order amount for CustomerID MAISD? How does that relate to our CustomerGroup boundaries?

Hint

Using "between" works well for integer values. However, the value we're working with is Money, which has decimals. Instead of something like:

```
when TotalOrderAmount between 0 and 1000 then 'Low'
```

You'll need to something like this:

```
when TotalOrderAmount >= 0 and TotalOrderAmount  < 1000 then 'Low'
```

50. Customer grouping with percentage

Based on the above query, show all the defined CustomerGroups, and the percentage in each. Sort by the total in each group, in descending order.

Expected Result

CustomerGroup	TotalInGroup	PercentageInGroup
Medium	35	0.432098765432
Low	20	0.246913580246
High	13	0.160493827160
Very High	13	0.160493827160

Hint

As a starting point, you can use the answer from the problem "Customer grouping—fix null".

Hint

We no longer need to show the CustomerID and CompanyName in the final output. However, we need to count how many customers are in each CustomerGrouping. You can create another CTE level in order to get the counts in each CustomerGrouping for the final output.

51. Customer grouping—flexible

Andrew, the VP of Sales is still thinking about how best to group customers, and define low, medium, high, and very high value customers. He now wants complete flexibility in grouping the customers, based on the dollar amount they've ordered. He doesn't want to have to edit SQL in order to change the boundaries of the customer groups.

How would you write the SQL?

There's a table called CustomerGroupThreshold that you will need to use. Use only orders from 2016.

Expected Result

Customer ID	Company Name	Total Order Amount	Customer Group Name
ALFKI	Alfreds Futterkiste	2302.20	Medium
ANATR	Ana Trujillo Emparedados y helados	514.40	Low
ANTON	Antonio Moreno Taquería	660.00	Low
AROUT	Around the Horn	5838.50	High
BERGS	Berglunds snabbköp	8110.55	High
BLAUS	Blauer See Delikatessen	2160.00	Medium
BLONP	Blondesddsl père et fils	730.00	Low
BOLID	Bólido Comidas preparadas	280.00	Low
BONAP	Bon app'	7185.90	High
BOTTM	Bottom-Dollar Markets	12227.40	Very High
BSBEV	B's Beverages	2431.00	Medium
CACTU	Cactus Comidas para llevar	1576.80	Medium
CHOPS	Chop-suey Chinese	4429.40	Medium
COMMI	Comércio Mineiro	513.75	Low
CONSH	Consolidated Holdings	931.50	Low
DRACD	Drachenblut Delikatessen	2809.61	Medium
DUMON	Du monde entire	860.10	Low
EASTC	Eastern Connection	9569.31	High
ERNSH	Ernst Handel	42598.90	Very High
FOLKO	Folk och fä HB	15973.85	Very High
FRANK	Frankenversand	5587.00	High

(The expected results are the same as for the original problem, it's just that we're getting the answer differently. The total rows returned will still be 81, we're just showing a subset here.)

As a starting point, use the SQL of the first CTE from the problem "Customer grouping with percentage"

```
Select
    Customers.CustomerID
    ,Customers.CompanyName
    ,TotalOrderAmount = SUM(Quantity * UnitPrice)
From Customers
    join Orders
        on Orders.CustomerID = Customers.CustomerID
    join OrderDetails
        on Orders.OrderID = OrderDetails.OrderID
Where
    OrderDate >= '20160101'
    and OrderDate  < '20170101'
Group By
    Customers.CustomerID
    ,Customers.CompanyName
```

Hint

When thinking about how to use the table CustomerGroupThreshold, note that when joining to a table, you don't need to only use an equi-join (i.e., "=" in the join). You can also use other operators, such as between, and greater than/less than (> and <).

52.   Countries with suppliers or customers

Some Northwind employees are planning a business trip, and would like to visit as many suppliers and customers as possible. For their planning, they'd like to see a list of all countries where suppliers and/or customers are based.

Expected Results

Country
Argentina
Australia

| Austria |
| Belgium |
| Brazil |
| Canada |
| Denmark |
| Finland |
| France |
| Germany |
| Ireland |
| Italy |
| Japan |
| Mexico |
| Netherlands |
| Norway |
| Poland |
| Portugal |
| Singapore |
| Spain |
| Sweden |
| Switzerland |
| UK |
| USA |
| Venezuela |

Hint

Use the Union statement for this. It's a good way of putting together a simple resultset from multiple SQL statements.

53. Countries with suppliers or customers, version 2

The employees going on the business trip don't want just a raw list of countries, they want more details. We'd like to see output like the below, in the Expected Results.

Expected Result

SupplierCountry	CustomerCountry
NULL	Argentina

Australia	NULL
NULL	Austria
NULL	Belgium
Brazil	Brazil
Canada	Canada
Denmark	Denmark
Finland	Finland
France	France
Germany	Germany
NULL	Ireland
Italy	Italy
Japan	NULL
NULL	Mexico
Netherlands	NULL
Norway	Norway
NULL	Poland
NULL	Portugal
Singapore	NULL
Spain	Spain
Sweden	Sweden
NULL	Switzerland
UK	UK
USA	USA
NULL	Venezuela

Hint

A good way to start would be with a list of countries from the Suppliers table, and a list of countries from the Customers table. Use either Distinct or Group by to avoid duplicating countries. Sort by country name

Hint

You should have something like this:

```
Select Distinct Country from Customers
Select Distinct Country from Suppliers
```

You can combine these with a CTEs or derived tables.

Note that there's a specific type of outer join you'll need, designed to return rows from *either* resultset. What is it? Look online for the different types of outer join available.

54.   Countries with suppliers or customers, version 3

The output in the above practice problem is improved, but it's still not ideal

What we'd really like to see is the country name, the total suppliers, and the total customers.

Expected Result

Country	TotalSuppliers	TotalCustomers
Argentina	0	3
Australia	2	0
Austria	0	2
Belgium	0	2
Brazil	1	9
Canada	2	3
Denmark	1	2
Finland	1	2
France	3	11
Germany	3	11
Ireland	0	1
Italy	2	3
Japan	2	0
Mexico	0	5
Netherlands	1	0
Norway	1	1
Poland	0	1
Portugal	0	2
Singapore	1	0
Spain	1	5
Sweden	2	2
Switzerland	0	2
UK	2	7
USA	4	13
Venezuela	0	4

Hint

You should be able to use the answer from the previous problem, and make a few changes to the CTE source queries to show the total number of Supplier countries and Customer countries. You won't be able to use the Distinct keyword anymore.

When joining the 2 CTEs together, you can use a computed column, with the IsNull function to show a non-null Country field, instead of the Supplier country or the Customer country.

55.   First order in each country

Looking at the Orders table—we'd like to show details for each order that was the first in that particular country, ordered by OrderID.

So, for each country, we want one row. That row should contain the earliest order for that country, with the associated ShipCountry, CustomerID, OrderID, and OrderDate.

Expected Results

ShipCountry	CustomerID	OrderID	OrderDate
Argentina	OCEAN	10409	2015-01-09
Austria	ERNSH	10258	2014-07-17
Belgium	SUPRD	10252	2014-07-09
Brazil	HANAR	10250	2014-07-08
Canada	MEREP	10332	2014-10-17
Denmark	SIMOB	10341	2014-10-29
Finland	WARTH	10266	2014-07-26
France	VINET	10248	2014-07-04
Germany	TOMSP	10249	2014-07-05
Ireland	HUNGO	10298	2014-09-05
Italy	MAGAA	10275	2014-08-07
Mexico	CENTC	10259	2014-07-18
Norway	SANTG	10387	2014-12-18
Poland	WOLZA	10374	2014-12-05
Portugal	FURIB	10328	2014-10-14
Spain	ROMEY	10281	2014-08-14
Sweden	FOLKO	10264	2014-07-24
Switzerland	CHOPS	10254	2014-07-11
UK	BSBEV	10289	2014-08-26
USA	RATTC	10262	2014-07-22
Venezuela	HILAA	10257	2014-07-16

Your first step will probably be to create a query like this:

```
Select
    ShipCountry
    ,CustomerID
    ,OrderID
    ,OrderDate = convert(date, OrderDate)
From orders
Order by
    ShipCountry
    ,OrderID
```

…which shows all the rows in the Order table, sorted first by ShipCountry and then by OrderID.

Your next step is to create a computed column that shows the row number for each order, partitioned appropriately.

There's a class of functions called Window functions or Ranking functions that you can use for this problem. Specifically, use the Row_Number() function, with the Over and Partition clause, to get the number, per country, of a particular order.

You'll have something like this:

```
Select
    ShipCountry
    ,CustomerID
    ,OrderID
    ,OrderDate = convert(date, OrderDate)
    ,RowNumberPerCountry =
        Row_Number()
            over (Partition by ShipCountry Order by ShipCountry, OrderID)
From Orders
```

Because of some limitations with Window functions, you can't directly filter the computed column created above. Use a CTE to solve the problem.

56.   Customers with multiple orders in 5 day period

There are some customers for whom freight is a major expense when ordering from Northwind.

However, by batching up their orders, and making one larger order instead of multiple smaller orders in a short period of time, they could reduce their freight costs significantly.

Show those customers who have made more than 1 order in a 5 day period. The salespeople will use this to help customers reduce their freight costs.

Note: There is more than one way of solving this kind of problem. This time, we will *not* be using Window functions.

Expected Result

Customer ID	Initial Order ID	Initial Order Date	Next Order ID	Next Order Date	Days Between Orders
ANTON	10677	2015-09-22	10682	2015-09-25	3
AROUT	10741	2015-11-14	10743	2015-11-17	3
BERGS	10278	2014-08-12	10280	2014-08-14	2
BERGS	10444	2015-02-12	10445	2015-02-13	1
BERGS	10866	2016-02-03	10875	2016-02-06	3
BONAP	10730	2015-11-05	10732	2015-11-06	1
BONAP	10871	2016-02-05	10876	2016-02-09	4
BONAP	10932	2016-03-06	10940	2016-03-11	5
BOTTM	10410	2015-01-10	10411	2015-01-10	0
BOTTM	10944	2016-03-12	10949	2016-03-13	1
BOTTM	10975	2016-03-25	10982	2016-03-27	2
BOTTM	11045	2016-04-23	11048	2016-04-24	1
BSBEV	10538	2015-05-15	10539	2015-05-16	1
BSBEV	10943	2016-03-11	10947	2016-03-13	2
EASTC	11047	2016-04-24	11056	2016-04-28	4
ERNSH	10402	2015-01-02	10403	2015-01-03	1
ERNSH	10771	2015-12-10	10773	2015-12-11	1

(Some rows were not included, the total should be 71)

Hint

You can use a self-join, with 2 instances of the Orders table, joined by CustomerID. Good naming for the table aliases (table instances) is important for readability. Don't name them Order1 and Order2.

Hint

```
Select
    InitialOrder.CustomerID
    ,InitialOrderID = InitialOrder.OrderID
    ,InitialOrderDate = InitialOrder.OrderDate
    ,NextOrderID = NextOrder.OrderID
    ,NextOrderDate = NextOrder.OrderDate
from Orders InitialOrder
    join Orders NextOrder
        on InitialOrder.CustomerID = NextOrder.CustomerID
Order by
    InitialOrder.CustomerID
    ,InitialOrder.OrderID
```

This is a good start. You will need to filter on additional fields in the join clause between InitialOrder and NextOrder, because as it is, this returns far too many orders. It has what's called a cartesian product between the 2 instances of the Orders table. This means that for the total number of orders for a particular customer in Orders, you'll have that number, squared, in the output.

Look at some of the OrderID and OrderDate values in InitialOrder and NextOrder. Some of them definitely disqualify a row based on our criteria.

Hint

Should the OrderID of the NextOrder ever be less than or equal to the OrderID of the InitialOrder?

Hint

Based on the hint above, we added a where clause.

```
Select
```

```
    InitialOrder.CustomerID
    ,InitialOrderID = InitialOrder.OrderID
    ,InitialOrderDate = InitialOrder.OrderDate
    ,NextOrderID = NextOrder.OrderID
    ,NextOrderDate = NextOrder.OrderDate
from Orders InitialOrder
    join Orders NextOrder
        on InitialOrder.CustomerID = NextOrder.CustomerID
where
    InitialOrder.OrderID < NextOrder.OrderID
Order by
    InitialOrder.CustomerID
    ,InitialOrder.OrderID
```

Adding this filter:

```
and InitialOrder.OrderID < NextOrder.OrderID
```

…has cut down the output a lot. However, we still need to filter for the 5 day period.

Create a new field called DaysBetween that calculates the number of days between the InitialOrder OrderDate and the NextOrder OrderDate. Use the DateDiff function.

Hint

You should now have a line like this:

```
DaysBetween = datediff(dd, InitialOrder.OrderDate, NextOrder.OrderDate)
```

Use this calculation in the Where clause to filter for 5 days or less between orders.

57.   Customers with multiple orders in 5 day period, version 2

There's another way of solving the problem above, using Window functions. We would like to see the following results.

Expected Results

CustomerID	OrderDate	NextOrderDate	DaysBetweenOrders

ANTON	2015-09-22	2015-09-25	3
AROUT	2015-11-14	2015-11-17	3
BERGS	2014-08-12	2014-08-14	2
BERGS	2015-02-12	2015-02-13	1
BERGS	2016-02-03	2016-02-06	3
BONAP	2015-11-05	2015-11-06	1
BONAP	2016-02-05	2016-02-09	4
BONAP	2016-03-06	2016-03-11	5
BOTTM	2015-01-10	2015-01-10	0
BOTTM	2016-03-12	2016-03-13	1
BOTTM	2016-03-25	2016-03-27	2
BOTTM	2016-04-23	2016-04-24	1
BSBEV	2015-05-15	2015-05-16	1
BSBEV	2016-03-11	2016-03-13	2
EASTC	2016-04-24	2016-04-28	4
ERNSH	2015-01-02	2015-01-03	1
ERNSH	2015-12-10	2015-12-11	1
ERNSH	2015-12-11	2015-12-15	4
ERNSH	2016-03-23	2016-03-26	3
ERNSH	2016-04-08	2016-04-13	5
FOLKO	2016-03-26	2016-03-27	1
FOLKO	2016-03-27	2016-04-01	5
FOLKO	2016-04-01	2016-04-06	5
FRANK	2015-09-16	2015-09-19	3

(Some rows were not included, the total should be 69)

Hint

The window function to use here is the Lead function.

Look up some examples of the Lead function online.

As a first step, write SQL using the Lead function to return results like the following. The NextOrderDate is a computed column that uses the Lead function.

Customer ID	Order Date	Next Order Date
ALFKI	2015-08-25	2015-10-03
ALFKI	2015-10-03	2015-10-13
ALFKI	2015-10-13	2016-01-15
ALFKI	2016-01-15	2016-03-16
ALFKI	2016-03-16	2016-04-09

ALFKI	2016-04-09	NULL
ANATR	2014-09-18	2015-08-08
ANATR	2015-08-08	2015-11-28
ANATR	2015-11-28	2016-03-04

Hint

You should have something like this:

```
Select
    CustomerID
    ,OrderDate = convert(date, OrderDate)
    ,NextOrderDate =
        convert(
            date
            ,Lead(OrderDate,1)
                OVER (Partition by CustomerID order by CustomerID, OrderDate)
            )
From Orders
Order by
    CustomerID
    ,OrderID
```

Now, take the output of this, and using a CTE and the DateDiff function, filter for rows which match our criteria.

What did you think of SQL Practice Problems?

First of all, thank you for purchasing this book. I know you have a lot of options for learning SQL, but you picked this book, and I am grateful that you did.

I hope that you learned useful SQL skills that will help you in your work. If you did, I would truly appreciate if you would post a review on Amazon. As an independent author with a marketing budget of zero, your review helps me tremendously, and also helps potential customers find SQL Practice Problems.

To write a review, you can go to the Amazon website, click on Orders in the top right, and find your order of SQL Practice Problems. Once you see your order, you'll find a link to write a product review.

Do you want more practice problems?

Please visit SQLPracticeProblems.com. It offers the Professional package which includes a completely new set of practice problems, as well as other bonus components including a no-hints edition and a MySQL edition.

Use the discount code **amazoncust** for a 50% discount on the Professional package.

Any feedback on the problems, hints, or answers? I'd like to hear from you. Please email me at feedback@SQLPracticeProblems.com.

ANSWERS

Introductory Problems

1.   Which shippers do we have?

```
Select
    *
From Shippers
```

Discussion

This is a basic select statement, returning all rows, just to get you warmed up.

Most of the time, a simple select statement like this is written all on one line, like this:

```
Select * From Shippers
```

But because we'll be getting more complex quickly, we'll start out with formatting it with separate lines for each clause, which we'll be doing in future questions.

2.   Certain fields from Categories

```
Select
    CategoryName
    ,Description
```

```
from Categories
```

Discussion

Instead of doing a "Select *", we specify the column names, and only get those columns returned.

3.   Sales Representatives

```
Select
    FirstName
    ,LastName
    ,HireDate
From Employees
Where
    Title = 'Sales Representative'
```

Discussion

This is a simple filter against a string datatype. When comparing a value to a string datatype, you need to enclose the value in single quotes.

What happens when you don't? Try running the following:

```
Select
    FirstName
    ,LastName
    ,HireDate
From Employees
Where
    Title = Sales Representative
```

Notice that SQL Server gives the error:

```
Incorrect syntax near 'Representative'.
```

What about if you compare against a number? Try the following:

```
Select
```

```
    FirstName
    ,LastName
    ,HireDate
From Employees
Where
    Title = 1
```

You should get a conversion failure error.

4.   Sales Representatives in the United States

```
Select
    FirstName
    ,LastName
    ,HireDate
From Employees
Where
    Title = 'Sales Representative'
    and Country = 'USA'
```

Discussion

You can have as many filters in the where clause as you need. I usually indent all the filters, and put them on new lines, in order to make it easier to read.

5.   Orders placed by specific EmployeeID

```
Select
    OrderID
    ,OrderDate
From Orders
Where
    EmployeeID = 5
```

This simple query filters for one value in the EmployeeID field, using the "=" comparison operator.

Here's another set of very commonly used comparison operators that you're probably familiar with from math class:

>	Greater than
<	Less than
>=	Greater than or equal to
<=	Less than or equal to

6. Suppliers and ContactTitles

```
Select
    SupplierID
    ,ContactName
    ,ContactTitle
From Suppliers
Where
    ContactTitle <> 'Marketing Manager'
```

Another way of expressing the Not is by using the following

!=

So, the below is equivalent to the answer with "<>".

```
Select
    CompanyName
    ,ContactName
    ,ContactTitle
From Suppliers
Where
    ContactTitle != 'Marketing Manager'
```

7. Products with "queso" in ProductName

```
Select
    ProductID
    ,ProductName
From Products
Where
    ProductName like '%queso%'
```

Discussion

The "Like" operator is always used with wildcards, such as the percent symbol (%), which substitutes for any number of characters.

Note that even though the search string used a lowercase "q" with the Like clause

```
ProductName like '%queso%'
```

the resulting rows both had an uppercase Q.

```
Queso Cabrales

Queso Manchego La Pastora
```

This is because the default installation of SQL Server is case insensitive, although it is also possible to have a case-sensitive installation.

8. Orders shipping to France or Belgium

```
Select
    OrderID
    ,CustomerID
    ,ShipCountry
From Orders
where
    ShipCountry = 'France'
    or ShipCountry = 'Belgium'
```

This is a very simple example, but in many situations you will have multiple where clauses, with combined "Or" and "And" sections.

In this situation, an alternative would have been to use the "In" operator. We'll do that in a future problem.

9.   Orders shipping to any country in Latin America

```
Select
    OrderID
    ,CustomerID
    ,ShipCountry
From Orders
where
    ShipCountry in
        (
        'Brazil'
        ,'Mexico'
        ,'Argentina'
        ,'Venezuela'
        )
```

Using the In statement like this is a very common scenario when writing SQL. Whenever there's more than just a few—say 2 or 3—values that we're filtering for, I will generally put them on separate lines. It's easier to read, understand, and modify.

Also, many times the list of items you're filtering for will be coming from somewhere else—for instance, a spreadsheet—and will already be on separate lines.

10.   Employees, in order of age

```
Select
    FirstName
    ,LastName
```

```
    ,Title
    ,BirthDate
From Employees
Order By Birthdate
```

Discussion

This is a simple example of an Order By clause.

By default, SQL Server sorts by ascending order (first to last). To sort in descending order (last to first), run the following, with the **desc** keyword:

```
Select
    FirstName
    ,LastName
    ,Title
    ,BirthDate
From Employees
Order By Birthdate desc   -- keyword desc for last to first search
```

11.   Showing only the Date with a DateTime field

```
Select
    FirstName
    ,LastName
    ,Title
    ,DateOnlyBirthDate = convert(date, BirthDate)
From Employees
Order By Birthdate
```

Discussion

What we're using here is called a computed column, also sometimes called a calculated column. Anytime you're doing something besides just returning the column, as it is stored in the database, you're using a computed column. In this case, we're applying a function to convert the datatype returned.

Note that we've added a name, DateOnlyBirthDate, for our computed column. This is called an "alias".

```
DateOnlyBirthDate = convert(date, BirthDate)
```

If you don't actually specify the column alias, you get an empty column header, which is not helpful.

12. Employees full name

```
Select
    FirstName
    ,LastName
    ,FullName = FirstName + ' ' + LastName
From Employees
```

Discussion

This is another example of a computed column. In this case, instead of applying a function to a field, we're concatenating two fields.

Another way to do concatenation, as of SQL Server 2012, is using the Concat function, as below.

```
Select
    FirstName
    ,LastName
    ,FullName = concat(FirstName , ' ' , LastName)
From Employees
```

The Concat function isn't very well known yet, since SQL programmers are more familiar with using the + operator to concatenate strings. However, there are benefits to using the Concat function, mainly when there are nulls in the data.

13. OrderDetails amount per line item

```
Select
    OrderID
    ,ProductID
    ,UnitPrice
```

```
    ,Quantity
    ,TotalPrice = UnitPrice * Quantity
From OrderDetails
Order by
    OrderID
    ,ProductID
```

Discussion

Here we have another example of a computed column, this time using the arithmetic operator "*" for multiplication.

A note on aliases—I believe the alias structure that I have above, with the alias name first and the computation after, is easiest to read.

However, you'll also very frequently see this structure, using "as":

```
Select
    OrderID
    ,ProductID
    ,UnitPrice
    ,Quantity
    ,UnitPrice * Quantity as TotalPrice    -- Alias using "as"
From OrderDetails
Order by
    OrderID
    ,ProductID
```

14.   How many customers?

```
Select
    TotalCustomers = count(*)
from Customers
```

Discussion

Aggregates functions and grouping are very important when retrieving data. In almost all cases, when doing data analysis, you'll be using multiple groupings and aggregates.

15. When was the first order?

```
Select
    FirstOrder = min(OrderDate)
From Orders
```

Discussion

For the aggregate function Count, you don't need to specify a column name—just count(*) will work.

However, for other aggregate functions such as Min, Avg, Sum, etc., you will need to specify a column name since you're not just counting all rows.

16. Countries where there are customers

```
Select
    Country
From Customers
Group by
    Country
```

Discussion

The Group By clause is a cornerstone of SQL. With most data analysis of any complexity at all, you'll be using multiple Group By clauses, so they're important to understand.

Another way of getting the same results is to use the Distinct keyword, as below:

```
Select distinct
    Country
From Customers
```

It looks simpler, and works well for queries that are very straightforward. But in everyday use, you'll use Group By more often than of Distinct, because you'll need to use additional aggregate functions such as Count, and Sum.

17.   Contact titles for customers

```
Select
    ContactTitle
    ,TotalContactTitle = count(*)
From Customers
Group by
    ContactTitle
Order by
    count(*) desc
```

Discussion

This particular construction, with a grouping, and then a count of the total in each group, is very common both on its own, and as a part of other queries.

18.   Products with associated supplier names

```
Select
    ProductID
    ,ProductName
    ,Supplier = CompanyName
From Products
    Join Suppliers
        on Products.SupplierID = Suppliers.SupplierID
```

Discussion

Joins can range from the very simple, which we have here, to the very complex. You need to understand them thoroughly, as they're critical in writing anything but the simplest SQL.

One thing you'll see when reading SQL code is, instead of something like the answer above, something like this:

```
Select
    ProductID
    ,ProductName
    ,Supplier = CompanyName
From Products P           -- Aliased table
    Join Suppliers S      -- Aliased table
```

```
    on P.SupplierID = S.SupplierID
```

Notice that the Products table and Suppliers table is aliased, or renamed, with one letter aliases—P and S. If this is done, the P and S need to be used in the On clause as well.

I'm not a fan of this type of aliasing, although it's common. The only benefit is avoiding some typing, which is trivial. But the downside is that the code is harder to read and understand.

It's not so much a problem in small chunks of SQL like this one. However, in long, convoluted SQL, you'll find yourself wondering what the one-letter aliases mean, always needing to refer back to the From clause, and translate in your head.

The only time I use tables aliases is if the table name is extremely long. And then, I use table alias names that are understandable, just shortened.

19.   Orders and the Shipper that was used

```
Select
    OrderID
    ,OrderDate = convert(date, OrderDate)
    ,Shipper =  CompanyName
From Orders
    join Shippers
        on Shippers.ShipperID = Orders.ShipVia
Where
    OrderID < 10270
Order by
    OrderID
```

Discussion

One common coding practice is to write the SQL as follows, with the table name (or alias) added to each column in the Select statement:

```
Select
    Orders.OrderID
    ,OrderDate = convert(date, Orders.OrderDate)
    ,Shipper =  Shippers.CompanyName
From Orders
```

```
    join Shippers
        on Shippers.ShipperID = Orders.ShipVia
Where
    Orders.OrderID < 10270
Order by
    Orders.OrderID
```

Notice that this SQL is identical to the SQL from the answer, except that it has a table name in front of every column name.

At some companies, this is the standard coding style, but I'm not a fan of it. I think it just makes the SQL longer, without improving the readability.

Intermediate Problems

20.   Categories, and the total products in each category

```
Select
    CategoryName
    ,TotalProducts = count(*)
From Products
    Join Categories
        on Products.CategoryID = Categories.CategoryID
Group by
    CategoryName
Order by
    count(*) desc
```

Discussion

We're expanding our knowledge of grouping here with a very common scenario—grouping across two joined tables. In this case, the tables have what's called a parent-child relationship. The parent table is Categories, and the child table is Products.

21.   Total customers per country/city

```
Select
    Country
    ,City
    ,TotalCustomers = Count(*)
From Customers
Group by
    Country
    ,City
Order by
    count(*) desc
```

Discussion

Note that once you have a Group by clause in a SQL statement, every field that appears in the Select statement needs to either appear in the Group by clause, or needs to have some kind of aggregate function applied to it.

For instance, try running the following, with the City in the Group by clause commented out, so we're no longer grouping by City.

```
Select
    Country
    ,City
    ,TotalCustomer = Count(*)
From Customers
Group by
    Country
    --,City
Order by
    count(*) desc
```

When you run this, you should receive this error message:

```
Msg 8120, Level 16, State 1, Line 3
Column 'Customers.City' is invalid in the select list because it is not contained in
either an aggregate function or the GROUP BY clause.
```

This means that the query engine doesn't know *which* City that you want to display. Every field in the Select clause needs to either have an aggregate function (like Sum, Count, etc.), or also be in the Group by. The reason behind this is that there could potentially be multiple different cities for any one value in the Country, and the database engine wouldn't know which one to show.

22. Products that need reordering

```
Select
    ProductID
    ,ProductName
    ,UnitsInStock
```

```
    ,ReorderLevel
From Products
Where
    UnitsInStock <= ReorderLevel
Order by ProductID
```

Discussion

This is a straightforward query on one table. Instead of using a string or numeric value to filter, we're using another field.

23.   Products that need reordering, continued

```
Select
    ProductID
    ,ProductName
    ,UnitsInStock
    ,UnitsOnOrder
    ,ReorderLevel
    ,Discontinued
From Products
Where
    UnitsInStock + UnitsOnOrder <= ReorderLevel
    and Discontinued = 0
Order by ProductID
```

Discussion

Instead of writing

```
and Discontinued = 0
```

...you can also write the following if you find it easier to read:

```
and Discontinued = 'false'
```

SQL Server will automatically convert the 'false' to 0.

24.   Customer list by region

```
Select
    CustomerID
    ,CompanyName
    ,Region
From Customers
Order By
    Case
        when Region is null then 1
        else 0
    End
    ,Region
    ,CustomerID
```

Discussion

Once the Case expression is set up correctly, you just need to create an Order By clause for it, and add the additional fields for sorting (Region and CustomerID).

If we needed to see the sorting field in the output, this would work:

```
Select
    CustomerID
    ,CompanyName
    ,Region
    ,RegionOrder=
        Case
        when Region is null then 1
        else 0
    End
From Customers
Order By
    RegionOrder
    ,Region
    ,CustomerID
```

You would not need to repeat the case statement in the Order By, you can just refer to the alias - RegionOrder.

25.   High freight charges

```
Select Top 3
    ShipCountry
    ,AverageFreight = Avg(freight)
From Orders
Group By ShipCountry
Order By AverageFreight desc
```

Discussion

Using Top is the easiest and most commonly used method of showing only a certain number of records. Another way is by using Offset, as below.

```
Select
    ShipCountry
    ,AverageFreight = AVG(freight)
From Orders
Group By ShipCountry
Order by AverageFreight DESC
OFFSET 0 ROWS FETCH FIRST 3 ROWS ONLY
```

26.   High freight charges—2015

```
Select Top 3
    ShipCountry
    ,AverageFreight = avg(freight)
From Orders
Where
    OrderDate >= '20150101'
    and OrderDate  < '20160101'
Group By ShipCountry
Order By AverageFreight desc
```

Discussion

An alternate way to write the where clause is this:

```
Where
    OrderDate >= '1/1/2015'
```

```
    and OrderDate   < '1/1/2016'
```

Depending on which date format you're used to, it may be easier to read. However, using the format YYYYMMDD will be correct worldwide, regardless of the DateFormat setting in SQL Server.

And here's still another way of writing this:

```
Select Top 3
    ShipCountry
    ,AverageFreight = avg(freight)
From Orders
Where
    year(OrderDate) = 2015            -- using Year function
Group By ShipCountry
Order By AverageFreight desc
```

This looks straightforward and is easy to read. However, when you put a function such as Year on the OrderDate field, we can't use the index anymore. Also, you can only filter for one specific calendar year instead of a range, so it's not very flexible.

27.   High freight charges with between

The OrderID that's causing the different results is 10806.

Discussion

There's an order made on December 31, 2015 with a really high value in the Freight field. This would have skewed the results, and put France in third place for highest freight charges, but only if it were included in the Where clause.

This SQL would have worked fine if OrderDate were a Date field, instead of DateTime.

```
OrderDate between '20150101' and '20151231'
```

However, since it's a DateTime field, it gives an incorrect answer because it's not taking into account records where the OrderDate is *during the day* on December 31, 2015.

Note that for a DateTime field, the value

```
'20151231'
```

is equivalent *only* to

2015-12-31 00:00:00.000

…and *not* to values that have a time component.

28. High freight charges—last year

```
Select TOP (3)
    ShipCountry
    ,AverageFreight = Avg(freight)
From Orders
Where
    OrderDate >= Dateadd(yy, -1, (Select max(OrderDate) from Orders))
Group by ShipCountry
Order by AverageFreight desc;
```

Discussion

Using SQL like this that can generate a dynamic date range is critical for most data analysis work. Most reports and queries will need to be flexible, without hard-coded date values.

29. Employee/Order Detail report

```
Select
    Employees.EmployeeID
    ,Employees.LastName
    ,Orders.OrderID
    ,Products.ProductName
    ,OrderDetails.Quantity
From Employees
    join Orders
        on Orders.EmployeeID = Employees.EmployeeID
    join OrderDetails
        on Orders.OrderID = OrderDetails.OrderID
    join Products
```

```
        on Products.ProductID = OrderDetails.ProductID
Order by
    Orders.OrderID
    ,Products.ProductID
```

This problem is more practice with basic joins and multiple tables.

You can replace Join with Inner Join, but most people just use Join.

30.   Customers with no orders

```
Select
    Customers_CustomerID = Customers.CustomerID
    ,Orders_CustomerID = Orders.CustomerID
From Customers
    left join Orders
        on Orders.CustomerID = Customers.CustomerID
Where
    Orders.CustomerID is null
```

There are many ways of getting the same results. The main options are the Left Join with Is Null, Not In, and Not Exists.

Above, we used the Left Join option. When performance is equivalent, I prefer the Not In method, shown below.

```
Select CustomerID
From Customers
Where
    CustomerID not in (select CustomerID from Orders)
```

I believe this is the easiest to read and understand.

Another option is to use Not Exists. This requires a correlated subquery.

```
Select CustomerID
From Customers
```

```
Where Not Exists
    (
    Select CustomerID
    from Orders
    where
        Orders.CustomerID = Customers.CustomerID
    )
```

Performance for the different options can be affected by whether or not the fields are indexed or nullable. For additional reading on the details, check out this article: NOT IN vs. NOT EXISTS vs. LEFT JOIN / IS NULL: SQL Server (https://explainextended.com/2009/09/15/not-in-vs-not-exists-vs-left-join-is-null-sql-server/).

31. Customers with no orders for EmployeeID 4

```
Select
    Customers.CustomerID
    ,Orders.CustomerID
From Customers
    left join Orders
        on Orders.CustomerID = Customers.CustomerID
        and Orders.EmployeeID = 4
Where
    Orders.CustomerID is null
Order by Customers.CustomerID
```

Discussion

Because the filters in the Where clause are applied after the results of the Join, we need the EmployeeID = 4 filter in the Join clause, instead of the Where clause.

Run the below query and review the results. It should give you a better sense of how the left join with "is null" works. Note that the Where clause is commented out.

```
Select
    Customers.CustomerID
    ,Orders.CustomerID
    ,Orders.EmployeeID
From Customers
```

```
left join Orders
    on Orders.CustomerID = Customers.CustomerID
    and Orders.EmployeeID = 4
-- Where
--    Orders.CustomerID is null
```

The most common way to solve this kind of problem is as above, with a left join. However, here are some alternatives using Not In and Not Exists.

```
Select CustomerID
From Customers
Where
    CustomerID not in (select CustomerID from Orders where EmployeeID = 4)

Select CustomerID
From Customers
Where Not Exists
    (
    Select CustomerID
    from Orders
        where Orders.CustomerID = Customers.CustomerID
        and EmployeeID = 4
    )
```

Yet another option for this answer is the Except statement. It's not as well known, because it was introduced relatively recently in SQL Server 2008. Also, there are some differences with the treatment of Nulls when using Except.

```
Select CustomerID From Customers
Except
Select CustomerID From Orders where EmployeeID = 4
```

Advanced Problems

32.   High-value customers

```
Select
    Customers.CustomerID
    ,Customers.CompanyName
    ,Orders.OrderID
    ,TotalOrderAmount = SUM(Quantity * UnitPrice)
From Customers
    Join Orders
        on Orders.CustomerID = Customers.CustomerID
    Join OrderDetails
        on Orders.OrderID = OrderDetails.OrderID
Where
    OrderDate >= '20160101'
    and OrderDate  < '20170101'
Group by
    Customers.CustomerID
    ,Customers.CompanyName
    ,Orders.Orderid
Having Sum(Quantity * UnitPrice) > 10000
Order by TotalOrderAmount DESC
```

Discussion

If you tried putting this filter

```
and sum(Quantity * UnitPrice)  >= 10000
```

… in the where clause, you got an error. Aggregate functions can only be used to filter (with some exceptions) in the Having clause, not the Where clause.

33.   High-value customers—total orders

```
Select
```

102

```
    Customers.CustomerID
    ,Customers.CompanyName
    --,Orders.OrderID
    ,TotalOrderAmount = SUM(Quantity * UnitPrice)
From Customers
    Join Orders
        on Orders.CustomerID = Customers.CustomerID
    Join OrderDetails
        on Orders.OrderID = OrderDetails.OrderID
Where
    OrderDate >= '20160101'
    and OrderDate  < '20170101'
Group by
    Customers.CustomerID
    ,Customers.CompanyName
    --,Orders.Orderid
Having sum(Quantity * UnitPrice) > 15000
Order by TotalOrderAmount desc
```

Discussion

All that was necessary here was to comment out references in the Select clause and the Group By clause to OrderID. By doing that, we're grouping at the Customer level, and not at the Order level.

34.   High-value customers—with discount

```
Select
    Customers.CustomerID
    ,Customers.CompanyName
    ,TotalsWithoutDiscount = SUM(Quantity * UnitPrice)
    ,TotalsWithDiscount = SUM(Quantity * UnitPrice * (1- Discount))
From Customers
    Join Orders
        on Orders.CustomerID = Customers.CustomerID
    Join OrderDetails
        on Orders.OrderID = OrderDetails.OrderID
Where
    OrderDate >= '20160101'
    and OrderDate  < '20170101'
```

```
Group by
    Customers.CustomerID
    ,Customers.CompanyName
Having sum(Quantity * UnitPrice * (1- Discount)) > 15000
Order by TotalsWithDiscount DESC
```

Discussion

Note that you need to use the new calculation for order totals with discounts in the Select clause, the Having clause, and also the Order by clause. In the Order by clause, you can re-use the alias that you created in the Select clause, but in the Having clause, you need to repeat the calculation.

35. Month-end orders

```
Select
    EmployeeID
    ,OrderID
    ,OrderDate
From Orders
Where OrderDate = EOMONTH(OrderDate )
Order by
    EmployeeID
    ,OrderID
```

Discussion

Very frequently the end of the month will be needed in queries and reports. The function EOMONTH was introduced in SQL Server 2012, so before that point, developers had to use a combination of functions like the below:

```
Where OrderDate = dateadd(month,1 + datediff(month,0,OrderDate),-1)
```

Here's a bonus question for you. There are actually 2 more orders where the OrderDate is the end of the month. They are OrderID 10806 and 10807.

Why are they not showing up in the results? Using a Convert or a Cast function, can you modify the SQL to show these 2 orders as well?

36.   Orders with many line items

```
Select top 10
    OrderID
    ,TotalOrderDetails = count(*)
From OrderDetails
Group By OrderID
Order By Count(*) desc
```

Discussion

Try switching to top 50 instead of top 10. What happens?

You'll notice that there are many orders that have 5 total line items. But since we originally only showed the top 10, SQL Server eliminated most of the orders with 5 line items.

If you want to show all of them, you can use the With Ties option as below:

```
Select top 10 with ties
    OrderID
    ,TotalOrderDetails = count(*)
From OrderDetails
Group By OrderID
Order By Count(*) desc
```

Note that the same query, with the "With Ties" keyword, now returns 37 rows because there are many rows with a value of 5 for TotalOrderDetails.

37.   Orders—random assortment

```
Select top 2 percent
    OrderID
From Orders
Order By NewID()
```

Discussion

The NewID() function creates a globally unique identifier (GUID). When you order by this identifier, you get a random sorting. In this case, we're using

```
top 2 percent
```

105

...to get the top 2 percent instead of a specific number of rows.

Using NewID() on a very large table may cause performance problems. Look up NewID online for details.

38.   Orders—accidental double-entry

```
Select
    OrderID
From OrderDetails
Where Quantity >= 60
Group By
    OrderID
    ,Quantity
Having Count(*) > 1
Order by
    OrderID
```

Discussion

This SQL shows orders that have at least 1 order detail with a quantity of 60 or more (the Where clause), *and* the quantity is duplicated within the order (the Group by and Having clause). This occurs because we're grouping on *both* OrderID and Quantity.

39.   Orders—accidental double-entry details

```
;with PotentialDuplicates as (
    Select
        OrderID
    From OrderDetails
    Where Quantity >= 60
    Group By OrderID, Quantity
    Having Count(*) > 1
    )
Select
    OrderID
    ,ProductID
```

```
    ,UnitPrice
    ,Quantity
    ,Discount
From OrderDetails
Where
    OrderID in (Select OrderID from PotentialDuplicates)
Order by
    OrderID
    ,Quantity
```

Discussion

There are quite a few different ways of getting the same results for this problem. Based on years of painful troubleshooting caused by poorly-written, tangled SQL, I suggest that writing easily understandable, straightforward code is one of the most important things to strive for. Using a well thought-out CTE is one way of doing this.

In the next problem, we'll look at another way of getting the same result.

40.   Orders—accidental double-entry details, derived table

```
Select
    OrderDetails.OrderID
    ,ProductID
    ,UnitPrice
    ,Quantity
    ,Discount
From OrderDetails
    Join (
        Select distinct
            OrderID
        From OrderDetails
        Where Quantity >= 60
        Group By OrderID, Quantity
        Having Count(*) > 1
    ) PotentialProblemOrders
        on PotentialProblemOrders.OrderID = OrderDetails.OrderID
Order by OrderID, ProductID
```

Discussion

Note the Distinct keyword, added after the Select in the derived table. This gives us only distinct rows in the output, which avoids the problem with duplicate OrderIDs.

41. Late orders

```
Select
    OrderID
    ,OrderDate = convert(date, OrderDate)
    ,RequiredDate = convert(date, RequiredDate)
    ,ShippedDate = convert(date, ShippedDate)
From Orders
Where
    RequiredDate <= ShippedDate
Order by
    OrderID
```

Discussion

This is a straightforward query that we'll use as a base for future problems.

42. Late orders—which employees?

```
Select
    Employees.EmployeeID
    ,LastName
    ,TotalLateOrders = Count(*)
From Orders
    Join Employees
        on Employees.EmployeeID = Orders.EmployeeID
Where
    RequiredDate <= ShippedDate
Group By
    Employees.EmployeeID
    ,Employees.LastName
Order by TotalLateOrders desc
```

Discussion

Note that both the LastName and the EmployeeID from the Employees table need to be included in the Group by clause, otherwise we get the error:

```
Msg 8120, Level 16, State 1, Line 3
Column 'Employees.LastName' is invalid in the select list because it is not
contained in either an aggregate function or the GROUP BY clause.
```

Technically, EmployeeID is a primary key field, and since we're grouping by that already, there can only be one LastName associated with an EmployeeID. However, the database engine doesn't know this, and still requires the LastName in the Group by clause.

43. Late orders vs. total orders

```
;With LateOrders as (
    Select
        EmployeeID
        ,TotalOrders = Count(*)
    From Orders
    Where
        RequiredDate <= ShippedDate
    Group By
        EmployeeID
)
, AllOrders as (
    Select
        EmployeeID
        ,TotalOrders = Count(*)
    From Orders
    Group By
        EmployeeID
)
Select
    Employees.EmployeeID
    ,LastName
    ,AllOrders = AllOrders.TotalOrders
    ,LateOrders = LateOrders.TotalOrders
```

```
From Employees
    Join AllOrders
        on AllOrders.EmployeeID = Employees.EmployeeID
    Join LateOrders
        on LateOrders.EmployeeID = Employees.EmployeeID
Order by Employees.EmployeeID
```

Discussion

The above query is almost correct, but if you're paying careful attention, you'll realize it has a slight problem. We'll learn more in the next problem.

Also, as usual there are different ways to get the same result. As a bonus exercise, you could try getting the same results another way, without CTE's and just using a Case statement to get total late orders.

44.   Late orders vs. total orders—missing employee

```
;With LateOrders as (
    Select
        EmployeeID
        ,TotalOrders = Count(*)
    From Orders
    Where
        RequiredDate <= ShippedDate
    Group By
        EmployeeID
)
, AllOrders as (
    Select
        EmployeeID
        ,TotalOrders = Count(*)
    From Orders
    Group By
        EmployeeID
)
Select
    Employees.EmployeeID
    ,LastName
    ,AllOrders = AllOrders.TotalOrders
```

```
    ,LateOrders = LateOrders.TotalOrders
From Employees
    Join AllOrders
        on AllOrders.EmployeeID = Employees.EmployeeID
    Left Join LateOrders
        on LateOrders.EmployeeID = Employees.EmployeeID
Order by Employees.EmployeeID
```

Discussion

If we wanted to show *all* employees, even if they had no orders, we would also have needed to use a Left Join for AllOrders.

45.   Late orders vs. total orders—fix null

```
;With LateOrders as (
    Select
        EmployeeID
        ,TotalOrders = Count(*)
    From Orders
    Where
        RequiredDate <= ShippedDate
    Group By
        EmployeeID
)
, AllOrders as (
    Select
        EmployeeID
        ,TotalOrders = Count(*)
    From Orders
    Group By
        EmployeeID
)
Select
    Employees.EmployeeID
    ,LastName
    ,AllOrders = AllOrders.TotalOrders
    ,LateOrders = IsNull(LateOrders.TotalOrders, 0)
From Employees
    Join AllOrders
```

```
        on AllOrders.EmployeeID = Employees.EmployeeID
    Left Join LateOrders
        on LateOrders.EmployeeID = Employees.EmployeeID
Order by Employees.EmployeeID
```

Discussion

Using a straightforward IsNull on LateOrder is the best way to solve this problem.

Another way to write it would be using a Case statement

```
LateOrders =
    Case
        When LateOrders.TotalOrders is null Then 0
        Else LateOrders.TotalOrders
    End
```

But when you don't need any other logic besides a test for null, IsNull is the way to go.

46.   Late orders vs. total orders—percentage

```
;With LateOrders as (
    Select
        EmployeeID
        ,TotalOrders = Count(*)
    From Orders
    Where
        RequiredDate <= ShippedDate
    Group By
        EmployeeID
)
, AllOrders as (
    Select
        EmployeeID
        ,TotalOrders = Count(*)
    From Orders
    Group By
        EmployeeID
)
Select
    Employees.EmployeeID
```

```
    ,LastName
    ,AllOrders = AllOrders.TotalOrders
    ,LateOrders = IsNull(LateOrders.TotalOrders, 0)
    ,PercentLateOrders =
        (IsNull(LateOrders.TotalOrders, 0) * 1.00) / AllOrders.TotalOrders
From Employees
    Join AllOrders
        on AllOrders.EmployeeID = Employees.EmployeeID
    Left Join LateOrders
        on LateOrders.EmployeeID = Employees.EmployeeID
Order by Employees.EmployeeID
```

Discussion

If you just add a field like this:

```
PercentLateOrders = LateOrders.TotalLateOrders/AllOrders.TotalOrders
```

…you'll get 0 for all the fields, which is obviously not correct. But this is what happens when you divide two integers together. You need to convert one of them to a data type such as decimal. A common way to convert to a decimal datatype is by multiplying by 1.00

Note that you need to convert the integer to a decimal *before* you do the division. If you do it after the division, like this:

```
(IsNull(LateOrders.TotalOrders, 0)  / AllOrders.TotalOrders) * 1.00
```

… you'll still get 0.

47. Late orders vs. total orders—fix decimal

```
;With LateOrders as (
    Select
        EmployeeID
        ,TotalOrders = Count(*)
    From Orders
    Where
        RequiredDate <= ShippedDate
    Group By
        EmployeeID
```

```
)
, AllOrders as (
    Select
        EmployeeID
        ,TotalOrders = Count(*)
    From Orders
    Group By
        EmployeeID
)
Select
    Employees.EmployeeID
    ,LastName
    ,AllOrders = AllOrders.TotalOrders
    ,LateOrders = IsNull(LateOrders.TotalOrders, 0)
    ,PercentLateOrders =
        Convert(
            Decimal (2,2)
            ,(IsNull(LateOrders.TotalOrders, 0) * 1.00) / AllOrders.TotalOrders
            )
From Employees
    Join AllOrders
        on AllOrders.EmployeeID = Employees.EmployeeID
    Left Join LateOrders
        on LateOrders.EmployeeID = Employees.EmployeeID
Order by Employees.EmployeeID
```

Discussion

Rounding, truncating, and converting data types can get complicated, and there are many ways that you could get unexpected results. Always check your results carefully, and know whether you want rounding, or truncation.

Frequently, when creating this kind of query, you'll put the output into a tool like Excel, and do any additional formatting such as setting the decimal precision there. However, it's good to at least know how to do it in SQL.

You may have noticed that I added some new lines in the calculation to make it easier to read. This isn't necessary, but it's good programming practice, and easier to read and troubleshoot compared to having everything on one line.

48. Customer grouping

```
;with Orders2016 as (
    Select
        Customers.CustomerID
        ,Customers.CompanyName
        ,TotalOrderAmount = SUM(Quantity * UnitPrice)
    From Customers
        Join Orders
            on Orders.CustomerID = Customers.CustomerID
        Join OrderDetails
            on Orders.OrderID = OrderDetails.OrderID
    Where
        OrderDate >= '20160101'
        and OrderDate  < '20170101'
    Group by
        Customers.CustomerID
        ,Customers.CompanyName
)
Select
    CustomerID
    ,CompanyName
    ,TotalOrderAmount
    ,CustomerGroup =
        Case
            when TotalOrderAmount between 0 and 1000 then 'Low'
            when TotalOrderAmount between 1001 and 5000 then 'Medium'
            when TotalOrderAmount between 5001 and 10000 then 'High'
            when TotalOrderAmount > 10000 then 'Very High'
        End
from Orders2016
Order by CustomerID
```

Discussion

(Note—there's a small bug in the above SQL, which we'll review in the next problem.)

The CTE works well for this problem, but it's not strictly necessary. You could also use SQL like this:

```
Select
    Customers.CustomerID
    ,Customers.CompanyName
```

```
        ,TotalOrderAmount = SUM(Quantity * UnitPrice)
        ,CustomerGroup =
            Case
                when SUM(Quantity * UnitPrice) between 0 and 1000 then 'Low'
                when SUM(Quantity * UnitPrice) between 1001 and 5000 then 'Medium'
                when SUM(Quantity * UnitPrice) between 5001 and 10000 then 'High'
                when SUM(Quantity * UnitPrice) > 10000 then 'Very High'
            End
From Customers
    Join Orders
        on Orders.CustomerID = Customers.CustomerID
    Join OrderDetails
        on Orders.OrderID = OrderDetails.OrderID
Where
    OrderDate >= '20160101'
    and OrderDate < '20170101'
Group By
    Customers.CustomerID
    ,Customers.CompanyName
```

This gives the same result, but notice that the calculation for getting the TotalOrderAmount was repeated 5 times, including the 4 times in the Case statement.

It's best to avoid repeating calculations like this. The calculations will usually be quite complex and difficult to read, and you want to have them only in one place. In something simple, like Quantity * UnitPrice, it's not necessarily a problem. But most of the time, you should avoid repeating any calculations and code. An easy way to remember this is with the acronym DRY, which stands for "Don't Repeat Yourself". Here's an article on the topic: https://en.wikipedia.org/wiki/Don%27t_repeat_yourself

49.   Customer grouping—fix null

```
;with Orders2016 as (
    Select
        Customers.CustomerID
        ,Customers.CompanyName
        ,TotalOrderAmount = SUM(Quantity * UnitPrice)
    From Customers
        Join Orders
```

```
            on Orders.CustomerID = Customers.CustomerID
        Join OrderDetails
            on Orders.OrderID = OrderDetails.OrderID
    Where
        OrderDate >= '20160101'
        and OrderDate  < '20170101'
    Group by
        Customers.CustomerID
        ,Customers.CompanyName
)
Select
    CustomerID
    ,CompanyName
    ,TotalOrderAmount
    ,CustomerGroup =
        case
            when TotalOrderAmount >= 0 and TotalOrderAmount  < 1000
                then 'Low'
            when TotalOrderAmount >= 1000 and TotalOrderAmount  < 5000
                then 'Medium'
            when TotalOrderAmount >= 5000 and TotalOrderAmount  <10000
                then 'High'
            when TotalOrderAmount >= 10000
                then 'Very High'
        end
from Orders2016
Order by CustomerID
```

Discussion

As you've been seeing in the above problems, knowing the data types you're working with and understanding the differences between them is important to get the right results. Using "between" would have been fine for integer values, but not for Money.

50. Customer grouping with percentage

```
;with Orders2016 as (
    Select
        Customers.CustomerID
```

```
            ,Customers.CompanyName
            ,TotalOrderAmount = SUM(Quantity * UnitPrice)
    From Customers
        join Orders
            on Orders.CustomerID = Customers.CustomerID
        join OrderDetails
            on Orders.OrderID = OrderDetails.OrderID
    Where
        OrderDate >= '20160101'
        and OrderDate  < '20170101'
    Group By
        Customers.CustomerID
        ,Customers.CompanyName
)
,CustomerGrouping as (
    Select
        CustomerID
        ,CompanyName
        ,TotalOrderAmount
        ,CustomerGroup =
            case
                when TotalOrderAmount >= 0 and TotalOrderAmount  < 1000
                    then 'Low'
                when TotalOrderAmount >= 1000 and TotalOrderAmount  < 5000
                    then 'Medium'
                when TotalOrderAmount >= 5000 and TotalOrderAmount  <10000
                    then 'High'
                when TotalOrderAmount >= 10000
                    then 'Very High'
            end
    from Orders2016
    -- Order by CustomerID
)
Select
    CustomerGroup
    , TotalInGroup = Count(*)
    , PercentageInGroup = Count(*) * 1.0/ (select count(*) from
CustomerGrouping)
from CustomerGrouping
group by CustomerGroup
order by TotalInGroup  desc
```

118

Discussion

In the answer we added an intermediate CTE called CustomerGrouping. CustomerGrouping is referenced twice—once to get the total number of customers in the group, and once to get the total, as the denominator for the percentage.

Notice that the Order by in the second CTE is commented out. If you leave it in, you get this error:

```
Msg 1033, Level 15, State 1, Line 32
The ORDER BY clause is invalid in views, inline functions, derived tables,
subqueries, and common table expressions, unless TOP, OFFSET or FOR XML is also
specified.
```

51.   Customer grouping—flexible

```
;with Orders2016 as (
    Select
        Customers.CustomerID
        ,Customers.CompanyName
        ,TotalOrderAmount = SUM(Quantity * UnitPrice)
    From Customers
        Join Orders
            on Orders.CustomerID = Customers.CustomerID
        Join OrderDetails
            on Orders.OrderID = OrderDetails.OrderID
    Where
        OrderDate >= '20160101'
        and OrderDate  < '20170101'
    Group by
        Customers.CustomerID
        ,Customers.CompanyName
)
Select
    CustomerID
    ,CompanyName
    ,TotalOrderAmount
    ,CustomerGroupName
from Orders2016
    Join CustomerGroupThresholds
        on Orders2016.TotalOrderAmount between
```

```
        CustomerGroupThresholds.RangeBottom and
CustomerGroupThresholds.RangeTop
Order by CustomerID
```

Discussion

Note that this gives the same results as the original problem. However, instead of using hard-coded values in the Case statement to define the boundaries of the CustomerGroups, you have them in a table.

The benefit of this is that you don't need to duplicate the following code in every query where you need to group customers, since it's defined in the table.

```
,CustomerGroup =
    case
        when TotalOrderAmount >= 0 and TotalOrderAmount  < 1000 then 'Low'
        when TotalOrderAmount >= 1000 and TotalOrderAmount  < 5000 then 'Medium'
        when TotalOrderAmount >= 5000 and TotalOrderAmount  <10000 then 'High'
        when TotalOrderAmount >= 10000 then 'Very High'
    end
```

Also, take a look at the values in CustomerGroupThresholds.

```
select * From CustomerGroupThresholds
```

Note that there's no overlap between the rows when you look at RangeBottom and RangeTop. If it were a data type besides Money (which goes to 4 decimal places), there might be gaps or overlap.

52.   Countries with suppliers or customers

```
Select Country From Customers
Union
Select Country From Suppliers
Order by Country
```

There are 2 ways of using the Union statement. One is a simple Union as in the answer here. Using a simple Union statement eliminates all the duplicates in the resultset.

You can also use Union All. Try it and take a look at the resultset:

```
Select distinct Country From Customers
Union All
Select distinct Country From Suppliers
Order by Country
```

Notice that within the individual SQL statements, I've put a Distinct. However, there are still duplicates in the final output, because we have Union All, which doesn't eliminate duplicates.

53.   Countries with suppliers or customers, version 2

```
;With SupplierCountries as
    (Select Distinct Country from Suppliers)
,CustomerCountries as
    (Select Distinct Country from Customers)
Select
    SupplierCountry = SupplierCountries .Country
    ,CustomerCountry = CustomerCountries .Country
From SupplierCountries
    Full Outer Join CustomerCountries
        on CustomerCountries.Country = SupplierCountries.Country
```

Discussion

The Full Outer join isn't commonly used, but in certain situations it's critical. Another way that these queries could have been joined is via a derived table, like below.

```
Select
    SupplierCountry = SupplierCountries .Country
    ,CustomerCountry = CustomerCountries .Country
```

```
From (Select Distinct Country from Suppliers) SupplierCountries
    Full Outer Join (Select Distinct Country from Customers) CustomerCountries
        on CustomerCountries.Country = SupplierCountries.Country
```

In this instance, you get the identical output to the CTE option, but I think the CTE option is easier to read.

Why are CTEs, in general, easier to read? The main reason is that the code can be more logically structured. It can be read from top to bottom without needing to jump around to different sections. See this article (http://www.essentialsql.com/non-recursive-ctes/) for more details.

Are CTEs always the answer? No, not always. The main case in which you should switch from a CTE to something else (for instance, a table variable or temporary table) would be when you need to reference the results of the select statement multiple times, in a longer piece of code.

54.   Countries with suppliers or customers, version 3

```
;With SupplierCountries as
    (Select Country , Total = Count(*) from Suppliers group by Country)
,CustomerCountries as
    (Select Country, Total = Count(*) from Customers group by Country)
Select
    Country = isnull( SupplierCountries.Country, CustomerCountries.Country)
    ,TotalSuppliers= isnull(SupplierCountries.Total,0)
    ,TotalCustomers= isnull(CustomerCountries.Total,0)
From SupplierCountries
    Full Outer Join CustomerCountries
        on CustomerCountries.Country = SupplierCountries.Country
```

Discussion

Note that we had to switch from Distinct to Group By in the CTE, because we needed to get the total with Count(*). You can't use Distinct in this situation.

The Full Outer type join is not very commonly used, but in some situations, it's the only syntax you can use that will get the results you need.

55. First order in each country

```
;with OrdersByCountry as
(
    Select
        ShipCountry
        ,CustomerID
        ,OrderID
        ,OrderDate = convert(date, OrderDate)
        ,RowNumberPerCountry =
            Row_Number()
                over (Partition by ShipCountry Order by ShipCountry, OrderID)
    From Orders
)
Select
    ShipCountry
    ,CustomerID
    ,OrderID
    ,OrderDate
From OrdersByCountry
Where
    RowNumberPerCountry = 1
Order by
    ShipCountry
```

Discussion

Before Window functions were available, in previous versions of SQL Server, there were other options to get the same results.

The below returns the same resultset as we got with the Row_Number() function:

```
;with FirstOrderPerCountry as (
    Select
        ShipCountry
        ,MinOrderID = min(OrderID)
    From Orders
    Group by
        ShipCountry)
Select
    Orders.ShipCountry
    ,CustomerID
    ,OrderID
```

```
from FirstOrderPerCountry
    Join Orders
        on Orders.OrderID = FirstOrderPerCountry.MinOrderID
Order by
    Orders.ShipCountry
```

However, what if we had wanted to order by something else such as ShippedDate? Since ShippedDate isn't a unique value like OrderID, we would not have been able to join on it.

There are workarounds for this issue, but a Window function is definitely easier.

56. Customers with multiple orders in 5 day period

```
Select
    InitialOrder.CustomerID
    ,InitialOrderID = InitialOrder.OrderID
    ,InitialOrderDate = convert(date, InitialOrder.OrderDate)
    ,NextOrderID = NextOrder.OrderID
    ,NextOrderDate = convert(date, NextOrder.OrderDate)
    ,DaysBetweenOrders = datediff(dd, InitialOrder.OrderDate,
NextOrder.OrderDate)
from Orders InitialOrder
    join Orders NextOrder
        on InitialOrder.CustomerID = NextOrder.CustomerID
where
    InitialOrder.OrderID < NextOrder.OrderID
    and datediff(dd, InitialOrder.OrderDate, NextOrder.OrderDate) <= 5
Order by
    InitialOrder.CustomerID
    ,InitialOrder.OrderID
```

Discussion

Including multiple instances of a table is one way of finding the answer we need.

When aliasing tables and columns, be careful to name them something meaningful, so that you can read and understand your SQL.

57. Customers with multiple orders in 5 day period, version 2

```
;With NextOrderDate as (
    Select
        CustomerID
        ,OrderDate = convert(date, OrderDate)
        ,NextOrderDate =
            convert(
                date
                ,Lead(OrderDate,1)
                    OVER (Partition by CustomerID order by CustomerID,
OrderDate)
                )
    From Orders
)
Select
    CustomerID
    ,OrderDate
    ,NextOrderDate
    ,DaysBetweenOrders = DateDiff (dd, OrderDate, NextOrderDate)
From NextOrderDate
Where
    DateDiff (dd, OrderDate, NextOrderDate)  <= 5
```

Discussion

There are two main ways of solving this problem. The first uses multiple instances of the table (which we did in the first version of the problem), and the other uses Window functions.

Which is better? If we're okay with getting a narrower resultset, I'd prefer this version, using the Lead window function, instead of the previous solution.

But if we need multiple columns from the following order, then it's best to use the first version. Otherwise, you'd need multiple calculated columns with the same Partition and Order by.

Notice that the row count between the 2 answers is slightly different, 71 and 69. One of the customers that causes this discrepancy is CustomerID ERNSH. Look at the results of the answer SQL from problem #56. Why would one OrderID show up twice?

Made in the USA
Las Vegas, NV
07 January 2024

84022578R00074